Table of Contents

Finding Main Idea

Learn About Finding Main Idea

Thinking about the strategy

The **main idea** of any reading selection is the most important point the author is trying to make. In fiction, the main idea is a truth about life that the author demonstrates by the story. The main idea of a story is also called the theme.

Suppose you complain you can't do something. Your dad says, "Once, I tried to fix my radio-controlled car. I replaced the battery, but nothing happened. Then without success, I checked the connections. Finally, I unlodged a pebble locking the wheel. My car worked!"

Problem: The car didn't work.
Solutions: replaced battery; checked connections; removed pebble
End Result: The car worked.
Main Idea: Keep trying, and you can solve a problem.

In fiction, as in the example above, you often have to figure out the main idea by looking at the main character's experiences. The main character solved the problem successfully after three attempts. So the idea "If you keep trying, you can solve a problem" fits the story.

Studying a model

Read the story and the notes beside it.

The Right One

The third sentence states a problem—the main character Betsey needs a white blouse and she wants a special one.

The real problem is that the blouse is sold.

Betsey's solution is to look further, not settle for a plain shirt.

The end result is that she finds the blouse she wants.

That she insists on finding the right blouse suggests the main idea: Persistence pays off.

Betsey lurched out of bed, dressed, and hurried to breakfast. "I want to be at the store when it opens, Mum," she said. "I want that white blouse with the pearly sequins for the band concert. I've saved enough money, and it's the only blouse that will do!"

Betsey's mother drove her to the mall. Betsey ran into the store and strode directly to the display. To her horror, the blouse was gone. Only dreadfully plain white shirts hung on the rack. The salesclerk explained that the last sequined blouse had sold yesterday.

Her mother suggested a plain shirt, but Betsey knew what she wanted. They browsed store after store in the mall, without luck. Her mother told her to give up. Then Betsey had an idea—the shop on Greene Street. Sure enough, Emma's Blouses had just the one Betsey was looking for, in just her size!

Learn About a Graphic Organizer

Understanding a problem/solution map

A **problem/solution map** helps you study the events and circumstances in a story so that you can figure out the main idea. Listing the problems shows you what issues the character is working with. Listing the solutions/outcomes of the problems and the end result reveals the author's message about the issues. If the character solves the problem well, the author is telling you that the character's actions (and/or other actions and events in the story) are beneficial. If the outcome is negative, the character may have done something wrong or faced something beyond control.

Look at this problem/solution map for the story on page 4.

Problems include the initial difficulty and all the pitfalls the character faces.

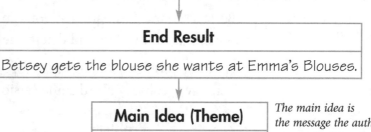

Problems	Solutions/Outcomes
Betsey needs a blouse. →	Betsey and Mum go shopping.
Betsey wants the right blouse. →	They go to a particular store.
The blouse is sold. →	Betsey wants to look further.
Mum suggests a plain shirt. →	Betsey refuses.
The blouse isn't in the mall. →	Betsey suggests Emma's Blouses.

Solutions/outcomes are the actions and the choices the character makes to try to solve the problems.

The end result is the last outcome—what happens at the end of the story.

End Result
Betsey gets the blouse she wants at Emma's Blouses.

Main Idea (Theme)
Persistence pays off.

The main idea is the message the author suggests by the end result.

A problem/solution map lays out the details of the story. You know that your statement of the main idea is supported by the details. You know why the author chose to have the events unfold as they did.

What details of the story suggest that persistence pays off?
Betsey tries different ways to get her blouse, and she succeeds.

As you read, ask yourself

- What is the most important, or main, idea?
- For nonfiction, is the main idea stated in the first or last sentence or the first or last paragraph?
- For fiction, what main idea, or theme, do the problems/solutions and the end result suggest?

Learn About a Form of Writing

A **fable** is a particular type of narrative, or story, that is related to myths, legends, folktales, and other folk literature. Fables are normally very short stories or poems with a moral as the main idea. The moral suggests how to find happiness or worth by living the way a good person does—or how to avoid trouble by not living the way a foolish or evil person does. Folk literature was a teaching tool of early peoples. Storytellers told the fables generation after generation to educate the young.

Fables have a few distinguishing characteristics.

- The characters are usually animals that talk and act like humans, but a person or an object may also be a main character.
- The story is not meant to be believed but rather read for its lesson about life.
- The main idea is the moral, or lesson about life. The moral is often stated at the end of the fable as a proverb such as "A stitch in time saves nine," or "A rolling stone gather no moss."
- The events can be unusual or unlikely, yet the story is told as though it is absolutely true.

Because a fable is a narrative, you can use a problem/solution map to examine the events of the story and determine the main idea, or moral lesson.

Here is a problem/solution map for Aesop's fable "The Tortoise and the Hare." You have probably heard some version of this story.

Problems	Solutions/Outcomes
Tortoise is angry about Hare's boasting and teasing. →	Tortoise answers Hare back.
Hare challenges Tortoise to race. →	Tortoise accepts.
Hare eats and naps. Tortoise keeps moving ahead. →	Hare falls behind.

End Result
Hare loses race.

Main Idea (Theme)
Slow and steady wins the race.

A problem/solution map for the fable shows how the events support the main idea, or moral lesson: If you move slowly and steadily, you can achieve more than a fast, overconfident person.

Prepare for the Reading Selection

Gaining knowledge

Fables existed as an oral tradition long before they were written down. Aesop (620–560 B.C.), a Greek slave, is credited with hundreds of fables that are still read today. Aesop's stories came from ancient sources as far away as India. In 300 B.C., Demetrius of Phaleron recorded the *Aesopic Tales*. Later, a 17th century French writer Jean de La Fontaine rewrote Aesop's simple fables into a series of very witty stories. Authors continue to rewrite Aesop's work even today.

In spite of the rewriting, the idea of a moral lesson has never been set aside. It defines a fable. Of course, a piece of literature always has a main idea— the theme. But the theme is not often stated in a story. The author presents characters, actions, and events to help the reader understand the theme, which is usually an observation, suggestion, or lesson about life. In a fable, the theme *is* the moral lesson—the correct or incorrect action of the characters and the result it brings. It is often stated as a proverb at the end of the story. A fable proverb refers to the story details but suggests a general lesson: for example, "A stitch in time saves nine" suggests "Take care of small problems so they don't grow big." If the main idea is not stated in the fable, it is never hard to figure out by looking at the evil and kind actions of the characters. Think about the lesson being taught in the fable on the following pages.

Learn Vocabulary

Understanding vocabulary

The boxed words below are **boldfaced** in the selection. Learn the meaning of each word. Then write the word beside its definition.

brackish	
spacious	
rashly	
exertion	
admonished	
exquisite	
abhorred	
cacophonous	
pruning	
palatable	

1. _____ having much space; roomy

2. _____ hated; rejected

3. _____ cautioned or warned; showed mild disapproval

4. _____ strenuous effort

5. _____ containing some salt; briny

6. _____ cutting back to improve growth

7. _____ having a harsh, discordant sound

8. _____ beautifully made or designed

9. _____ acceptable to the taste; agreeable

10. _____ without due thought or caution

Read the first part of the fable "The Price of Idleness."

The Price of Idleness

Crocodiles usually know what is good for them. They live in shallow, sometimes **brackish**, rivers, or among the freshwater weeds in open swamps. They float, alert, nostrils above water and eyes just breaking the surface as they scan for a tasty turtle or fish (or you and I) to eat. That is the truth for most crocodiles.

But one young crocodile found his marshy life boring and tasteless. He even disliked catching his food. He became so restless that he fussed daily to his parents. Yet, he did nothing.

"You have a choice, son," his frustrated father declared.

"What choice? I'm a crocodile!" he wailed resentfully.

His mother responded, "Yes, dear, you are. But I've heard them say (whoever they are) that a tiger or leopard or something can change its stripes or spots or something. So stop being lazy and solve your problem."

The young crocodile pondered these sage words. Then he stood up on his rear legs (a formidable 12 feet tall) and walked into a town. No one questioned the crocodile because—well—who would question a strolling crocodile? He searched for a place to begin a new life. He found a white four-room cottage near a field. This seemed a pleasant place to raise a family. But he had come alone. So he decided that tomorrow he would go back to the marshes to find a wife.

The next morning, he bought the cottage from a real-estate agent (who didn't even ask for references!). Then the crocodile walked back to the marshes and sat on the bank, crying crocodile tears. (You have heard of them, I presume?) A kind young crocodile swam up to him. "Why are you crying?" the pretty crocodile asked.

"I am so lonely in my lovely white cottage by the fertile field. I want a wife and a family. I need someone to decorate the four **spacious** rooms," the crocodile moaned.

Now the young lady crocodile had never dreamed of living in a white cottage near a fertile field (how many crocodiles have?) so she immediately, and a bit **rashly**, offered to live with him as his wife.

He smiled broadly, pleased with his success. "Good! I shall never be lonely or bored again." (And if Mrs. Crocodile had not done such a splendid job of decorating . . .)

The next Sunday, all across the marsh, hundreds of eyes peered out as a fidgety crow married Mr. and Mrs. Crocodile. Her parents cried as their daughter set off toward the white cottage with her new husband.

"I fear she will be greatly disappointed," her mother mourned.

"She will do what she has to do," her father commented.

After the wedding, Mr. and Mrs. Crocodile walked through the town to the white cottage. No one questioned the young couple because—well—who would question *two* strolling crocodiles!

Mrs. Crocodile set about decorating the tiny cottage, inside and out. Mr. Crocodile never offered to help. She painted the walls in the bedrooms and got him a feather bed. She put plants in each room and got a comfy chair. When she hung wallpaper in the dining room, he supervised from the chair. Mrs. Crocodile discovered that she was extremely fond of plants. So fond, indeed, that she planted a huge garden: a blush of colorful flowers among green vegetable vines in the fertile field.

Mr. Crocodile was very content with his new life. He had a wife. Soon baby crocodiles would be swimming in the bathtub of the cottage bathroom. His loving wife had adorned his home so beautifully that he found himself spending more and more time inside. He had reached for what he wanted, and life was perfect.

Completing a problem/solution map

This is a problem/solution map for the first part of the fable. Some of the map has been filled in. Add more information. Then read the end result and the main idea.

Problems		Solutions/Outcomes
Mr. Crocodile is bored with life.	→	He complains and fusses.
His parents speak to him.	→	He goes out to find a new place to live.
He feels lonely.	→	
	→	
	→	
	→	

End Result

He has a new type of life in a lovely cottage with a fine wife.

Main Idea (Theme)

If you reach for what you want, you can get it.

Read the second part of the fable "The Price of Idleness."

Mrs. Crocodile spent hours in her yard, tending her garden. She wanted a moat for swimming outside, but Mr. Crocodile was too happy inside his little cottage to help. So she dug it herself. She enjoyed the **exertion**, the fresh air and sunshine, the rain and the clouds, while her husband stayed cocooned in the cottage.

She planned a special pool to raise their young. Mr. Crocodile refused to help, saying that the bathtub was good enough. Then he sat back and lazily stared at his tiny bathtub for an hour or more. So Mrs. Crocodile dug a hole, lined it with smooth stones, and filled it with water. In the vegetation next to the pool, she laid her eggs.

Mr. Crocodile was a little annoyed at this "wild" behavior. But, when the children hatched, he was sure they'd love his bathroom. So he stayed inside and waited. Days past. At first, he wandered from room to room, staring out the windows and peering at the garden and the moat and the trees beyond the field. Then he walked from room to room, without looking outside. He felt less and less like going out. Soon, he hardly left his own room; he lay in bed for hours. One day, he asked Mrs. Crocodile to close the blind so that he would not be distracted by the riot of color outside the window.

"Life in this cottage is just what I wanted," he reminded his wife.

Mrs. Crocodile **admonished** him, "Yes my love, but you don't do anything and you stay inside too much! Why don't you come out to my pool and meet our children! You will find the air fresh and pleasing; you will find the sun cheerful; you will feel healthy and young, as I do."

Mr. Crocodile stared at her from his bed, blankets pulled to his eyes. "Why should I leave this comfy little cottage?" he asked.

"Because there is a world out there: trees and bugs and clouds and sunshine and rain and your children!" Mrs. Crocodile insisted.

"Oh, it's such an effort! Can't you bring them to my bathtub—the children, that is?"

"They are happy outside, as I am!" Mrs. Crocodile exclaimed.

"Well, I suppose I *can* come out." He slipped out of bed and tucked his back legs into alligator slippers. He put a huge straw hat atop his head and pulled it over his eyes.

Excitedly, Mrs. Crocodile waved her arms about as she showed her husband her **exquisite** landscaping. She pointed to the half-grown crocodiles. "Listen to them splash! Young crocodiles belong outside, my dear. And so do you! Why, hear the bees and the wind!"

But Mr. Crocodile now **abhorred** being outside. "It's far too wild outside! Look at those growing plants and that oozy water! Hear those horrid bees making a **cacophonous** racket!" Frantically, he rushed in, stumbling over a rock. Once in his bedroom, he pulled the blankets up over his eyes. "I am much happier and healthier inside my perfect cottage," he said. He smiled, but it was a weak smile.

In the days that followed, Mr. Crocodile rarely left his bed and almost never his bedroom. His wife, still devoted, made sure he had food and water. But she spent most of her time outside, **pruning** and planting, gathering seeds for the next season, and most importantly playing in the pool with her growing children. She stayed young and healthy and joyful. But Mr. Crocodile lay in his bed, grinning, wishing for the sound of children (and a wife for that matter) inside his cottage. Perhaps he *should* join them outside. But his self-satisfied laziness had weakened him horribly, and he could no longer get up. He had turned as pale as a whitewashed olive, and his life was as **palatable** as the olive pit.

Using a problem/solution map

Fill in the problem/solution map to help you find the main idea, or theme, of the second part of the fable. The moral lesson is different than it seemed in the first part of the fable. Ask yourself, "What point is the author really trying to show?"

Problems	Solutions/Outcomes
→	
→	
→	
→	
→	

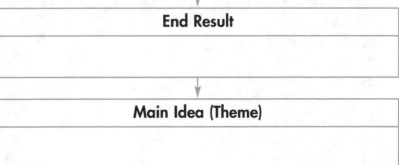

End Result

Main Idea (Theme)

Check Your Understanding

Think about what you've read. Then answer these questions.

1. Which of these is the best statement of the moral lesson of the fable?
   - Ⓐ Life can be really difficult when you don't do what you're supposed to do.
   - Ⓑ You can reach for what you want, but if you get lazy and stop growing and changing, you can get stuck.
   - Ⓒ Being a crocodile is not a pleasant way to live a life.
   - Ⓓ Always go with your first choice; people will respect you and you will have a perfect life.

2. If the fable ended after the first part, which title would best suggest the main idea?
   - Ⓐ "Crocodile Tears Win the Day"
   - Ⓑ "Crocodile's Pleasing New Life"
   - Ⓒ "Crocodiles Invade the Town"
   - Ⓓ "Living a Life in the Wild"

3. Brackish water would most likely be found
   - Ⓐ in a reservoir.
   - Ⓑ near the seacoast.
   - Ⓒ in an inland swamp.
   - Ⓓ in a rapidly flowing river.

4. Suppose you enter a small monkey cage at the zoo, and it is filled with noisy, howling monkeys. Which word might you use to describe the scene?
   - Ⓐ palatable
   - Ⓑ pruning
   - Ⓒ cacophonous
   - Ⓓ spacious

5. Which word is a synonym of *well-designed*?
   - Ⓐ exquisite
   - Ⓑ admonished
   - Ⓒ exertion
   - Ⓓ abhorred

6. At the start of the fable, why does the young crocodile decide to live on land?
   - Ⓐ He thinks life in the water is dull.
   - Ⓑ He hates marshy places and is afraid of water.
   - Ⓒ His parents treat him unkindly.
   - Ⓓ He has been offered a fine cottage in the country.

7. In the first part of the fable, what happens right after Mr. Crocodile realizes he has no family?
   - Ⓐ He walks back to the marshes to find a wife.
   - Ⓑ He buys the cottage from a real-estate agent.
   - Ⓒ He searches around for a cottage to live in.
   - Ⓓ He sits at the edge of the marshes, crying.

8. The main purpose of the fable is
   - Ⓐ to teach the reader a truth about life.
   - Ⓑ to explain examples of good behavior.
   - Ⓒ to describe an impossible incident.
   - Ⓓ to entertain the reader with a silly story.

9. Consider the last sentence in the fable: "He had turned as pale as a whitewashed olive, and his life was as palatable as the olive pit." What is meant by the phrase *palatable as the olive pit*?
   - Ⓐ His life was a bit agreeable, in the same way that the pit is a small part of the olive.
   - Ⓑ His life could improve, since the pit has the seed of the olive.
   - Ⓒ His life had lost its taste and pleasure, in the same way that the pit is not good to eat.
   - Ⓓ His life is filled with problems caused by the olives his wife feeds him.

10. Mrs. Crocodile is different from her husband because she
    - Ⓐ spends no time in the cottage.
    - Ⓑ never wanted to live in a cottage.
    - Ⓒ keeps herself busy mostly outside the cottage.
    - Ⓓ doesn't like the cottage they live in.

11. What do you think would happen if the fable continued?

Ⓐ Mrs. Crocodile would give up her work outside and stay inside to nurse her sick husband.

Ⓑ The young crocodiles would agree to come into the bathtub to cheer up their father.

Ⓒ Mr. and Mrs. Crocodile would live happily for many years, as they have been.

Ⓓ Mr. Crocodile would continue to grow weaker and weaker.

12. Why is Mr. Crocodile weak at the end of the story?

Ⓐ He has led a difficult life, struggling to survive on land.

Ⓑ He has worked too hard, building moats, pools, and gardens for his wife.

Ⓒ He has stopped doing anything useful.

Ⓓ He gets no food or water because he stays inside all the time.

Extend Your Learning

- *Write Your Own Fable*

    Use a problem/solution map to plan a fable. Start with the main idea, or moral lesson you want to teach. Choose a simple idea about life that is meaningful to you. Then outline the problems, solutions/outcomes, and end result that could teach that lesson. Use your plans to write your fable. Add at least one drawing. When you are finished, read your fable to a group. Have the group determine your main idea. If they are wrong, try to find out why. Does your fable need more work? Did the listeners miss an important outcome?

- *Perform a Play*

    Work in groups to select a fable by Aesop or another fable writer, such as Jean de La Fontaine, Rudyard Kipling, James Thurber, Joel Chandler Harris, and so on. Rewrite the fable as a play. Then have group members learn the roles, make props and costumes, and design the set. Present the play to the class.

- *Solve Your Own Problems*

    Think about a problem you have. Set it up in a problem/solution map similar to the one you used in this lesson. State your problem. Then list a possible solution. Follow through to an end result. Then state what that solution and end result might teach you or someone else—the main idea. Repeat the same procedure for the same problem with several other possible solutions, end results, and main ideas. Consider using this technique whenever you have a problem to solve.

Recalling Facts and Details

Learn About Recalling Facts and Details

Thinking about the strategy

Facts and details support the main idea in a reading selection. So to understand the main idea, you need to recall the facts and details. In nonfiction, the facts provide information about the main idea. In fiction, the details about characters, places, and events reflect the main idea the author is suggesting.

Here is a story beginning about school: At 8:00 A.M., the bell rang. Lee hurried to class. By 8:05, he was seated. Announcements began at 8:10. But the day really started with first class, math, at 8:15.

Bell	Seated at desk	Announcements	Math class
8:00 A.M.	8:05 A.M.	8:10 A.M.	8:15 A.M.

Sometimes, in fiction or nonfiction, the facts or details are presented with dates or times—*when*—as in the example above. Sometimes the facts and details are about *who, what, where, why,* or *how* something happens.

Studying a model

Read the story and the notes beside it.

Volcano!

The first sentence tells you when (May 14, 1980) and where (Mount St. Helens).

The following sentences give more details about who (speaker, family, aunt, officer), where (cottage, aunt's house,) when (May 4 to June 18), what (warnings, evacuation, eruption) and why (volcano erupts).

Wednesday, May 14, 1980, the scientists announced again that Mount St. Helens was rumbling. We had heard such news since about March 1, but the mountain had not erupted for 123 years. We got a formal warning on May 15. But my family had been at our mountain cottage since May 4, and it seemed as peaceful as ever.

On Friday afternoon, we heard sirens, and an officer knocked on our cottage door. "For your safety, you must leave now!"

We packed up a few things on Saturday and abandoned our cottage. (What can you take in such a case?) By Sunday, we were settled—if you could call it that—at my aunt's house 50 miles away. That was very lucky! Sunday morning, May 18, the volcano awoke. A bulge on the side collapsed, and a massive eruption blew off almost half the mountain. My aunt's house shook. We choked on the smoke, and ash-filled air. A second smaller eruption occurred on May 30. Sadly, we saw the ruins of our cottage in a TV news report on June 18. There was nothing there but ash—and more ash.

Learn About a Graphic Organizer

Understanding a timeline

A **timeline** normally plots events using a scale, such as 1 inch equals 2 years. When you use a timeline in reading, your scale does not need to be so exact. A timeline can help you organize and recall time-related details in some stories and nonfiction writings. If the details are given in chronological order, the timeline shows the events in story order. If the details are not given chronologically, the timeline helps you sort them out. The timeline helps you visualize when events occurred.

Look at this timeline for the first paragraph of the story on page 14. It includes all the important story details that lead up to the family's abandoning their cottage.

Each time increment, such as a month or year, is of equal length.

The time increment is labeled on the timeline.

Each entry lists the date and the event.

The events may be short sentences or phrases.

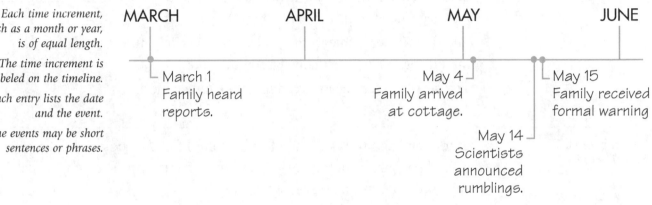

A timeline displays the relationship of details in time. You can better remember the events and circumstances in this way. You can more easily answer specific questions about places, causes, effects, experiences, ideas, and sequences, for example.

Did the family know Mount St. Helens had been active before they moved into the cottage? Yes, reports had been issued March 1, two months before the family arrived on May 4.

As you read, ask yourself

- What time-related details help clarify the events or information?
- Do facts and details tell *who, what, when, where, why,* or *how*?
- What specific details reveal the people, places, or things?

Learn About a Form of Writing

Fiction is "an imaginary creation in writing." This is the opposite of nonfiction, "writing that presents actual facts and/or true events." Short stories, novels, plays, ballads, and more are all forms of fiction. **Historical fiction** is a particular type of fiction that recreates the past. All the events are true-to-life even if they did not really happen.

Look for these characteristics to help identify historical fiction.

- Historical fiction is always set in a past time.
- Historical fiction makes use of some major event(s) or time period(s) in history.
- Some events in the story actually occurred, but the details surrounding them are exaggerated or invented by the author.
- The characters are true-to-life, and some, especially minor ones, may be famous people who actually lived at the time.
- The details of setting are accurate for the time period.

The story on page 14 is an example of historical fiction. Look at the second and third paragraphs of this story. Then study the timeline showing the details in time order, or chronological order.

MAY 1980	JUNE 1980	JULY 1980

May 16
told to leave

May 17
packed
and moved

May 18
settled at
aunt's house

volcano erupted

May 30
volcano
erupted again

June 18
saw TV report

A timeline is a very useful device for recalling details in historical fiction. You easily see how the events are related in time. Completing and studying a timeline can help you answer test questions or write essays about chronological information.

Prepare for the Reading Selection

Gaining knowledge

Historical fiction enables writers to go back to a time before they lived. Creating a story about the past, however, requires research. The author needs to learn how people lived at the time and to study the details of time and place, such as speech, dress, values, customs, beliefs, and common feelings. If the event is recent, the author may be able to question people who were there. For an earlier event, the author may read accounts written by participants or others who lived at the time. (Interviews, writings, and records from firsthand observers are called *primary sources*.) However, the author often has to base the story on writings such as nonfiction studies by history scholars. (These are *secondary sources*.)

On the following pages, you will read a historical fiction account of the 16th century voyage of Ferdinand Magellan. Of course, there is no one alive today who took this voyage. But one sailor, a nobleman named Antonio Pigafetta, kept a secret diary, which he later published. This diary has helped scholars to recreate the voyage, and historical fiction writers to weave stories around the facts.

Learn Vocabulary

Understanding vocabulary

The boxed words below are **boldfaced** in the selection. Learn the meaning of each word. Then write the word that could replace the underlined words in the sentence.

javelins
thwarting
mutiny
disembark
headwinds
mutineer
buffeted
vengefully
logs

1. _____ I begged to <u>get off the ship</u> and explore the island.

2. _____ The <u>records of the voyage</u> detailed our trip.

3. _____ <u>Winds blowing at our front</u> made progress slow.

4. _____ The <u>person trying to overthrow the leader</u> escaped.

5. _____ The injured dog attacked <u>with a desire for revenge</u>.

6. _____ Kim kept <u>making sure I didn't follow through on</u> my plans.

7. _____ Guards stopped the <u>open rebellion against authority</u>.

8. _____ We practiced throwing the <u>light, hand-held spears</u>.

9. _____ Strong waves <u>struck forcefully against</u> our ship.

Read the first part of the historical fiction story "360° West."

360° West

I learned that the contract with King Charles of Spain was signed long before we left. That was when Ferdinand Magellan, the man who would become my Captain-General, began preparations. His plan was to sail west across the Ocean Sea, through a strait nicknamed *el paso*, and onward to the Spice Islands. He gathered five small wooden ships, too old and worn to be worth a glance by most sailors. But with repairs, they would have to do. To make them seaworthy took over a year, I'm told.

By August 9, 1519, sailors had loaded the ships with tons of sea biscuits, salted beef and pork as well as cheese, rice, onions, flour, and barrels of water and wine. Magellan also geared the vessels with cannons, lances, swords, arrows, crossbows, **javelins**, and armor—as well as 5,000 pounds of gunpowder.

I signed on late, having by chance met Magellan. I longed to see the very great and awful things of the ocean. In the end, about 265 men joined the Captain-General on this voyage. I waited with great eagerness to depart.

Our first attempt to sail ceased when Magellan found supplies missing. He paused to resupply. Finally, on September 20, 1519, we sailed south into the Ocean Sea. I felt honored that Magellan had accepted me on the *Trinidad*, his lead ship. We were followed by the *San Antonio, Concepción,* and *Victoria*, whose Spanish captains neither trusted nor respected Magellan from the start. The fifth small ship, the *Santiago*, was captained by Magellan's friend Serrano. (It was lucky he had a few such friends.)

After seven days, we reached Tenerife, in the Canary Islands. It was there that the Captain-General learned, by an urgent letter from his father-in-law, that the three Spanish captains were plotting to kill him. Our wise Captain-General kept **thwarting** their evil plans!

We sailed along the African coast. Gazing at the water, I observed fierce sharks with terrible teeth. Soon, thunderstorms boomed, and mammoth waves bounced the ships like sticks in the sea. Saint Elmo's fire flashed on the masts. This calmed the sailors, for they saw it as a good omen. Yet when the lights were about to leave, so dazzling was the brightness that we remained for more than an eighth of an hour blinded, and calling for mercy.

The wind died except for sudden storms that swirled up yet carried us nowhere. Three weeks we waited for a current to carry us into the wind. On November 20, we crossed the equator and could no longer see the North Star. How that frightened the sailors! Yet Magellan bravely led us west toward new lands.

A second attempt on Magellan's life came swiftly—and failed. Next, one Spanish captain unwisely refused to follow orders, so he was rightfully accused of **mutiny** and put in chains.

With joy, we sighted our first new land on November 29. But Magellan would not let us sail near shore, nor **disembark**, until he found the safe harbor a friend had told him of. On December 13, we entered this glorious harbor. Natives in canoes surrounded the ships to greet us, peacefully, we hoped. These natives, I soon learned, had fierce customs, but they treated us as friends, traded with us, provided food, and even built us a house. We stayed until December 26, resting and repairing the ships.

Quite soon after we set off again, we sighted land with a western-facing coast. We believed we were at *el paso*, the passage through the continent that our Captain-General had promised!

Completing a timeline   This is a timeline of the important dates and events for the first part of the historical fiction story. Some information has been filled in. (Note that the September 27 date was not stated but had to be figured from "after seven days.") Add the missing dates and events.

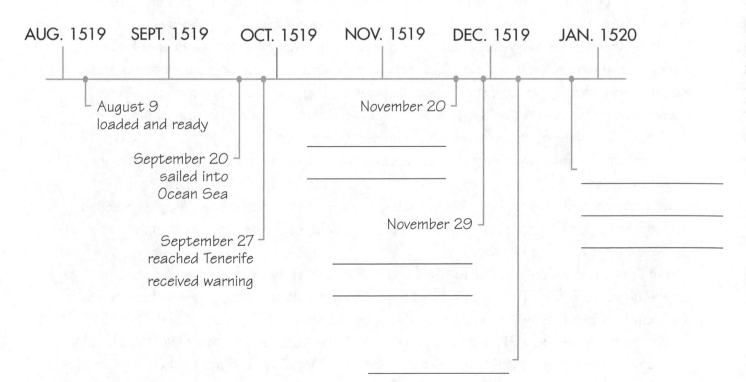

AUG. 1519   SEPT. 1519   OCT. 1519   NOV. 1519   DEC. 1519   JAN. 1520

August 9
loaded and ready

September 20
sailed into
Ocean Sea

September 27
reached Tenerife
received warning

November 20

November 29

Read the second part of the historical fiction story "360° West."

But alas, this was not *el paso*, though for weeks Magellan tried to prove it so. Disappointed, fearful, and tired, many sailors wanted to turn back. Still, Magellan insisted upon heading south to find a true passage. The Spanish captains, hoping to cause trouble, called a meeting. Our Captain-General pleaded well with his sailors, who agreed to press on with him. We sailed south February 3, 1520.

For weeks, the sea grew even colder. Stiff **headwinds** sometimes blew us backwards. Yet the Captain-General paused to explore every bay and inlet. The *Victoria* ran aground. The mast of the *Santiago* smashed. The *San Antonio* sprang a leak. Our clothes iced into brittleness, and then icebergs menaced the ships. Wisely, Magellan sailed into a cold, gray harbor on March 31. He named the spot San Julián, and it is there we spent the winter.

But the three Spanish captains secretly planned to sail home. They seized three ships. After much conflict, Magellan schemed to have the leader killed. Then he hung one **mutineer**, a murderer; others had to stand waist-deep in icy water and repair the ships. The *Santiago* went south to explore, and never returned.

Near San Julián, I saw strange beings. Flightless birds climbed stiffly on the icy rocks, looking like odd geese with black back feathers and white in front. Sea-wolf creatures with large teeth and no visible legs looped gracefully around the ships. Once, a giant man, friendly enough, suddenly appeared. More giants, which we named Patagonians, also arrived. Sadly, the crew tried to capture one: thus ended our friendly relations.

On October 18, 1520, with three new loyal captains, Magellan led the fleet onto a cold, dark, stormy sea. In two days, two ships set off to explore an inlet; they disappeared in a violent storm. When they at last returned, they swore they had found *el paso*. Yet when Magellan sent the *San Antonio* to check, it vanished. Since we found no sign of it nor shipwreck, we believed it had turned for home.

Storms and huge waves **buffeted** the ships as we navigated the narrow strait. At night, native fires dotted the shores, so we called the land *Tierra de los Fuegos*. Then, on November 28, we entered the unknown sea. At first it was calm and blue; Magellan called it Mar Pacifico. We hurried northwest to escape the cold, and then west, expecting to reach the Spice Islands in three or four days.

But this Mar Pacifico was not so small a sea. For months, we sailed without sight of a single inhabited island. These days, filled with fear, grave illness, and gnawing hunger, were the most horrible. Finally, the only sailor strong enough to climb the mast yelled, "Praise God! Land! Land!" As we neared land, in our weak state, we were robbed by natives. We headed to another island. Here natives rushed alongside, and Magellan recognized their language! He had been on these islands—the Philippines—long before. There was great friendship and sharing with the natives for a time. But Magellan, in a rage that some natives would not convert to Christianity, led us in attack. On April 27, he fell dead, stabbed by natives' spears.

The Spanish captains now took over **vengefully** and burned Magellan's **logs**. (I kept my diary hidden and later published it to expose the traitors.) We set out in two of the ships, and the captains behaved like pirates. On November 8, 1521, we reached the Spice Islands. In their greed, the captains overloaded the *Trinidad*, which began to leak. The *Victoria* set sail on February 21, 1522. On September 6, 1522, just 18 of us reached Spain. We few had achieved the dream of our Captain-General, and sailed west around the world.

Using a timeline   Use the timeline to list the important details of the second part of the historical fiction story.

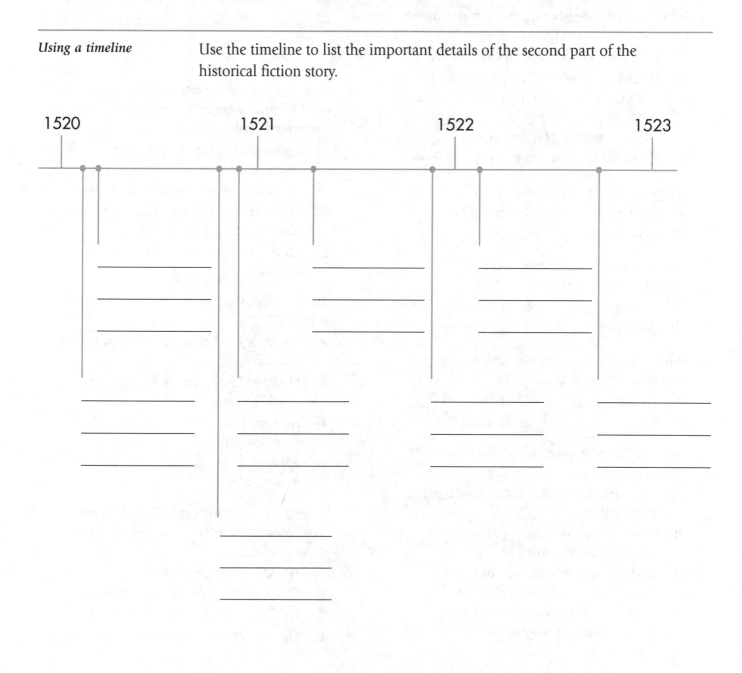

1520   1521   1522   1523

Check Your Understanding

Think about what you've read. Then answer these questions.

1. How long was the entire voyage around the world?
   - Ⓐ fourteen days more than one year
   - Ⓑ almost two years
   - Ⓒ two weeks short of three years
   - Ⓓ fourteen days short of two years

2. Which detail suggests that the narrator of the story was loyal to Magellan?
   - Ⓐ He signed on late after a chance meeting.
   - Ⓑ He believed, when they had reached a western-facing coast, that they had found the passage.
   - Ⓒ He kept a diary of the voyage.
   - Ⓓ He published his diary after the voyage.

3. A javelin is a
   - Ⓐ sailing tool.
   - Ⓒ container.
   - Ⓑ type of gun.
   - Ⓓ spear.

4. Which word means the opposite of "to get aboard a ship"?
   - Ⓐ buffeted
   - Ⓒ mutiny
   - Ⓑ disembark
   - Ⓓ thwarting

5. Which word completes the analogy?
   actor:play::mutineer:____
   - Ⓐ javelin
   - Ⓒ headwind
   - Ⓑ log
   - Ⓓ mutiny

6. What is the main purpose of this historical fiction story?
   - Ⓐ to inform the reader about how natives killed Magellan
   - Ⓑ to persuade the reader to dislike the Spanish captains
   - Ⓒ to describe the hardships of these historical voyages of exploration
   - Ⓓ to entertain the reader with a story of some historic importance

7. Which statement does not contain an opinion?
   - Ⓐ Yet the Captain-General paused to explore every bay and inlet.
   - Ⓑ We set out in two of the ships, and the captains behaved like pirates.
   - Ⓒ It was lucky he had a few such friends.
   - Ⓓ These days, filled with fear, grave illness, and gnawing hunger, were the most horrible.

8. How did Magellan's attack of the natives on the Philippines differ from his earlier encounters with natives?
   - Ⓐ Usually, he ignored natives who approached him.
   - Ⓑ Normally, he was friendly to natives.
   - Ⓒ Often, he steered his ships away from places occupied by natives.
   - Ⓓ Most times, he attacked natives with cannons.

9. The main idea of this historical fiction story is that
   - Ⓐ the voyage, with loss of life and hardship, did succeed.
   - Ⓑ Magellan never reached his goal because he died.
   - Ⓒ captains face many problems on sea voyages.
   - Ⓓ a long sea voyage causes people to act badly.

10. According to the historical fiction story, what caused Magellan to winter his fleet in San Julián?
    - Ⓐ His sailors begged him to.
    - Ⓑ The Spanish captains demanded it.
    - Ⓒ He faced icebergs and severe cold.
    - Ⓓ He was tired of arguing with his men.

11. The animals the narrator describes in the fourth paragraph on page 20 are most likely
    Ⓐ pigeons and sharks.
    Ⓑ seagulls and wolves.
    Ⓒ penguins and seals.
    Ⓓ snakes and wild dogs.

12. What happened in October 1520 after the two ships set off to explore an inlet?
    Ⓐ Giants arrived.
    Ⓑ The *San Antonio* disappeared.
    Ⓒ The ships got lost in a storm.
    Ⓓ Magellan began navigating the strait.

Extend Your Learning

- *Write Historical Fiction*

  Work with a group to pick an event or time in history, such as a battle of the Civil War, the invention of a useful product, or the Colonial period. Research in social studies texts, encyclopedias, library books, videos, and/or on the internet to gather information about your topic. Then write a historical fiction story of someone's experience at the time. Draw pictures to depict your story, add a timeline, and read your story to other groups.

- *Order Your Life*

  Create a timeline that orders and lists the important events in your life. You may include favorite school years, sports activities, vacations, visits, concerts, lessons, achievements, and awards. Design your timeline so that you can add to it as more events occur.

- *Research Explorers*

  In small groups, choose another explorer, such as Columbus, Dias, Cabot, Cartier, Verrazano, da Gama, Cabral, Vespucci, or Balboa, and find out more about his explorations. Write a short report highlighting something important or unusual about the person. Include a timeline of major events in the explorer's life. When all the groups are finished, create a master timeline of the major accomplishments.

Understanding Sequence

Learn About Understanding Sequence

Thinking about the strategy

Sequence is another word for order. When you think of sequence, you most often think of time order, or chronological order. In stories, sequence is the order in which the events happen. In an experiment or a recipe, it is the order in which the steps are done.

The author of a story may not always tell about events in the exact order that they happened. Events may jump around in time. For example, the author may talk about something that happened earlier: The girl didn't realize that before she arrived at class, the teacher had assigned new homework. Some events may happen at the same time: Just as I touched the doorknob, the door flew open.

Time-order sequence is often marked by sequence clue words that suggest the order such as *first, next, second, third, last, before, after,* and *finally*. The author may give dates and times that help you determine sequence.

In stories, notice how the sequence of events flows from beginning to middle to end. You will begin to see why certain events happen based on what has come before. You will be better able to predict what follows.

Studying a model

Read the story and the notes beside it.

A Simple Change

The first sentence tells you the first event.

The other events follow, signaled by words and phrases: first, second garden, next, fourth garden.

One clear morning, Mother Earth decided to take a walk. First she strolled into her rainforest garden. Huge ferny bushes provided soft shade. Multicolored orchids added grace and beauty to the tall trees. The second garden she visited was her temperate forest garden. Wildflowers grew plentifully at the base of bright sunlit green trees. Next, she entered her desert garden. The cactus plants stood tall and thick.

When she slid open the gate to the fourth garden, she spied a tree she had planted that was sadly withering. Such a thing had never happened before! So she set about checking for problems and watering the tree.

Suddenly, a huge frog crawled from behind the trunk. The frog pulled the tree up by its roots and stuck it back into the ground, branches first. Before he did that, he said, "I think you will find that this will solve the problem!" Over time, the tree grew tall, with abundant fruit and flowers.

In the end, the tree thrives.

But a few of the stems looked suspiciously like roots.

Learn About a Graphic Organizer

Understanding a sequence chain

A **sequence chain** helps you organize the events in a story. The chain begins with the first event in time, lists the middle events, and ends with the last event. When the events in the story are already in chronological, or time order, the sequence chain displays them in the same order as the author did. But often, the events are not given in order in the reading selection. The author may describe the past or hint at the future, and then go on with the narrative in the present. As you place the events in the sequence chain, you see when each event really occurred.

You will find time order in many types of reading selections, including fiction (such as short stories, novels, plays, and ballads) and nonfiction (such as biographies, experiments, personal accounts, recipes, how-to articles, and directions.)

Look at this sequence chain for the story on page 24. It lists, in time order, the events of the story. For this short story, every event is listed in a short sentence or phrase. For longer selections, you would pick only the most important events and list them as notes and phrases rather than sentences.

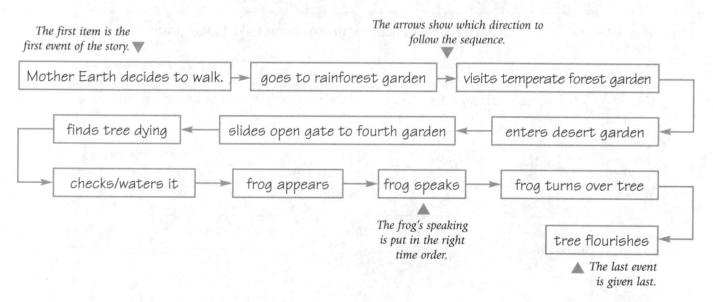

The first item is the first event of the story. ▼

The arrows show which direction to follow the sequence. ▼

Mother Earth decides to walk. → goes to rainforest garden → visits temperate forest garden

finds tree dying ← slides open gate to fourth garden ← enters desert garden

checks/waters it → frog appears → frog speaks → frog turns over tree

▲ *The frog's speaking is put in the right time order.*

tree flourishes

▲ *The last event is given last.*

A sequence chain shows how one event leads to the next. You can see the true order of events, even when they are presented in a different order in the story.

When did the frog speak to Mother Earth?
Before the frog turned over the tree.

As you read, ask yourself

• What happens first, next, finally?
• Are there sequence clue words, dates, and times to help you understand the sequence?

25

Learn About a Form of Writing

Focusing on a folktale

When humans first began creating fictional stories, these oral narratives were most likely either myths or **folktales**—or the two mixed together. Myths explain how the world was created or how human life began on earth. They are often religious or spiritual. Folktales suggest the themes of how to live, what to think, what to believe, or why things are as they are.

These are some of the characteristics of a folktale.

- A folktale is usually a narrative.
- A folktale relates to the folklore of everyday people—the values, beliefs, customs, superstitions, ideals, or legends.
- The main character is a person or an animal who talks.
- The main character faces a problem that is sorted out by the end of the folktale—either positively or negatively.
- Supernatural characters and events may appear.

Organizing ideas in a sequence chain

Study the sequence chain for the common folktale *Rumpelstiltskin*.

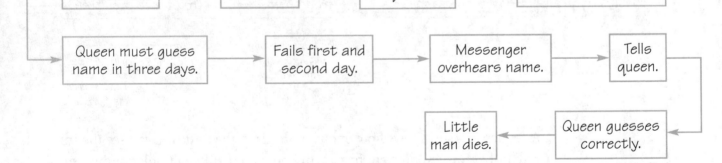

The sequence chain shows you the events in the story in the correct order. This makes it easy to remember and answer questions about the story.

Prepare for the Reading Selection

Gaining knowledge

The earliest folktales in North America are those of the native people, the hundreds of groups of American Indians who inhabited the continent long before Europeans arrived. Like all early people, Native Americans passed along stories orally to their children. Each tale usually taught a lesson or tried to explain something about nature or the world. The main character was often an animal with human characteristics that also had the ability to think and scheme. One familiar character in Native-American folktales is Coyote, a sometimes wise, frequently mischievous creature, who has been credited with a wide variety of adventurous deeds. You will read about one of the more notable of these deeds on the pages that follow.

Learn Vocabulary

Understanding vocabulary

The boxed words below are **boldfaced** in the selection. Learn the meaning of each word. Then write the word that matches the definition.

aggression
potential
succumbed
qualms
cohorts
lapse
frigid

1. _____ uncertain feelings that come from a guilty conscience

2. _____ a break in a regular pattern

3. _____ hostile or threatening action directed at others

4. _____ lacking warmth or heat; very cold

5. _____ what one might achieve in the future

6. _____ members of a group who all support one leader

7. _____ died from a disease, injury, or other hardship

Read the first part of the folktale "Coyote Brings Fire to Humans."

Coyote Brings Fire to Humans

Long ago, the People of Earth included all the creatures of land, sea, and sky. The newest and least knowledgeable among these People were humans. And even though humans had not exhibited signs of **aggression** toward any other living creature, there were those among the People who felt threatened by humans. So, in order to ensure that humans never realized their **potential** power, these People kept some important secrets from them. One of the greatest of these secrets was fire, which was carefully guarded by the three fierce Fire Holders.

Fur coats and thick hides kept the rest of the People warm when temperatures dropped. So until this time, no one cared that the Fire Holders would not share fire. Humans, of course, did not have fur or hide. Their very first winter on Earth, many humans, especially the very old and the very sick, **succumbed** to the icy, frigid temperatures. The next spring, when the ground softened, hundreds of humans were buried.

Coyote, who was the leader of all the People, felt no enmity toward humans. On the contrary, he felt sympathy for what they had suffered. One warm, sunny autumn day, Coyote overheard a group of woman weeping and chanting. "Oh, if only winter would not come. We cannot stand the bitter cold. How many among us will live to see another spring? How many of our children will survive to walk among the fields of summer flowers? Oh, if only People had a way to capture the sun's rays and bring its warmth indoors."

Coyote could not capture the sun's rays, but he could help the humans stay warm. He could bring them fire. Since the Fire Holders would not willingly share fire with anyone, Coyote would have to steal it from them. It had long been determined that the Fire Holders were being selfish so Coyote felt no **qualms** about his intentions. Nor did he feel bad enlisting the aid of Chipmunk and Frog. He also would need the help of one of the little boy humans. This child had learned Coyote's language and would be able to tell the rest of the humans what to do with fire when the time came. But first, Coyote and his friends would have to go to the mountain where the Fire Holders lived and steal the fire. So they sat down and mapped out their plan.

Completing a sequence chain

Study the sequence chain for the first part of the folktale. Then complete the chain by adding the other events of the story.

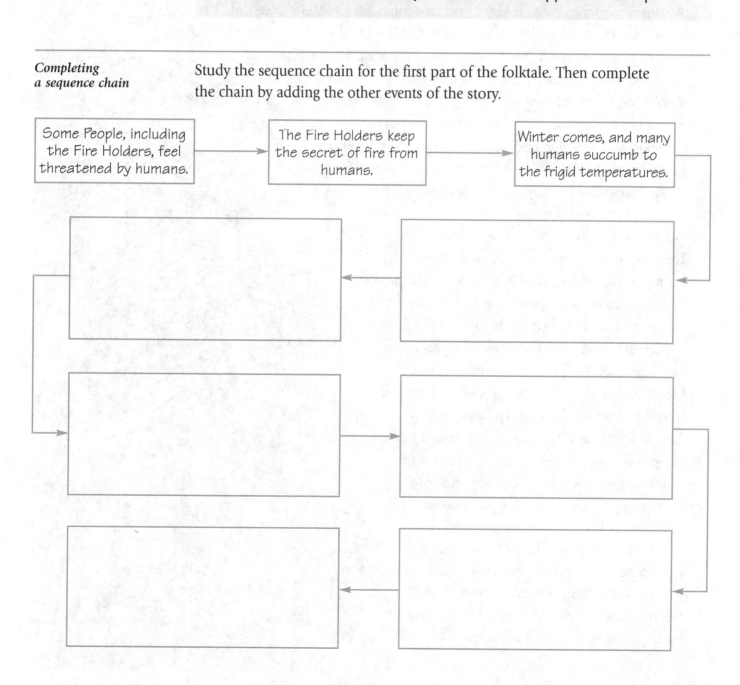

Some People, including the Fire Holders, feel threatened by humans. → The Fire Holders keep the secret of fire from humans. → Winter comes, and many humans succumb to the frigid temperatures.

Reading Selection—Part Two

Read the second part of the folktale "Coyote Brings Fire to Humans."

Coyote and his **cohorts** climbed the base of the mountain where the Fire Holders had their camp. According to the plan they had made, Chipmunk and Frog each took their place at different spots up the side of the mountain. Meanwhile, the little boy human waited with a piece of wood at the base of the mountain.

When everyone was at their appointed station, Coyote climbed all the way up to the Fire Holders' camp.

Earlier, Coyote had surveyed the camp for a couple of days to learn the Fire Holders' routine. He had noticed that each day at the exact moment of sunset, all three Fire Holders had gone into their tent. Coyote didn't know the reason why they had left the fire unguarded at sunset, and he didn't really care. He just knew that this **lapse** would give him the opportunity he needed. As he circled the Fire Holders' camp, he did not try to conceal himself. When the Fire Holders saw him, they were not concerned. "It's just an old coyote," they said, knowing that coyotes had no use for fire. When sunset came, all three disappeared into their tent as before.

At that moment, Coyote dashed toward the fire and grabbed a large spark. The Fire Holders heard the fire hiss and ran out of their tent. The first of them ran after Coyote. Her fiery hot fingers reached for Coyote and scorched his tail. Coyote was able to get away, but to this day the tip of his tail is ash white.

Coyote tossed the fire down the mountain to Chipmunk. Chipmunk began to run, but the second Fire Holder caught up to him and raked her three razor-sharp fingers down Chipmunk's back. Chipmunk screamed and flung the fire to Frog. To this day, the three black stripes down Chipmunk's back are his badge of courage. Frog jumped as fast and as far as he could. The third Fire Holder stepped down hard on Frog's tale, breaking it off. To this day, adult frogs have no tail. Frog got away and tossed the fire down to the little boy human, who held up the wood to catch the spark.

The Fire Holders did not know how to get fire from wood, so they gave up and returned to their camp. The little boy human carried the wood with the fire inside back to his village. The day before, Coyote had given him careful instructions about how to get fire from the wood by rubbing dry pieces of wood together. The little boy human showed his villagers how to do this. That winter was unusually **frigid**, but the humans were warm and lived to welcome spring.

Using a sequence chain   Use the sequence chain to list the events of the second part of the folktale. You may add more arrows and lines if you need them.

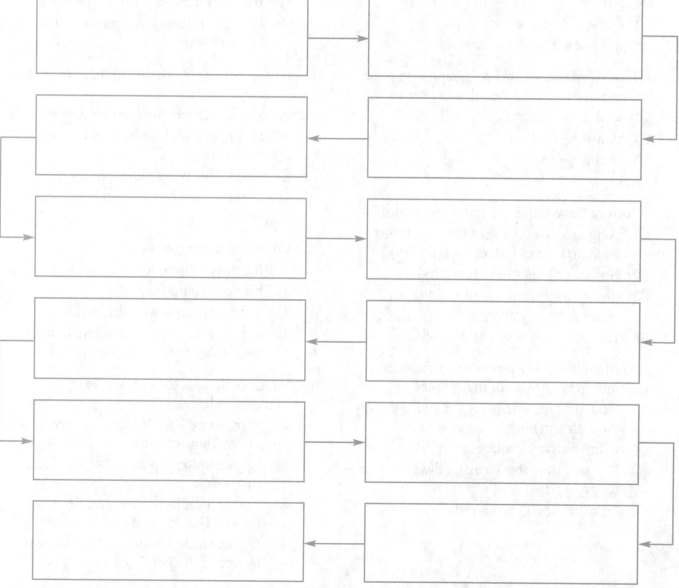

Check Your Understanding

Think about what you've read. Then answer these questions.

1. Which word completes the analogy?
   friendliness:harmony::aggression: _____
   - (A) conflict
   - (B) peace
   - (C) discussion
   - (D) power

2. If someone succumbed to an injury, most likely they
   - (A) avoided getting hurt.
   - (B) fell.
   - (C) could not bear to look at it.
   - (D) did not survive.

3. Which word in the third paragraph on page 28 provides a clue to the meaning of *enmity*?
   - (A) leader
   - (B) sympathy
   - (C) chanting
   - (D) capture

4. Which of these sentences states an opinion?
   - (A) Long ago, the People of Earth included all the creatures of land, sea, and sky.
   - (B) Humans did not have fur or hide.
   - (C) Coyote overheard a group of women weeping and chanting.
   - (D) The Fire Holders were being selfish.

5. According to the story, how are humans different from the rest of the People?
   - (A) Humans are more powerful and, therefore, more threatening.
   - (B) Humans live in villages.
   - (C) Humans don't have a natural way to stay warm.
   - (D) Humans don't keep secrets.

6. Which of these words are synonyms?
   - (A) cohorts, partners
   - (B) potential, weakness
   - (C) lapse, sleep
   - (D) frigid, heated

7. Which of these events happens first?
   - (A) Coyote teaches the little boy human how to get fire from wood.
   - (B) Coyote surveys the Fire Holders' camp.
   - (C) The boy catches the fire in the wood.
   - (D) The Fire Holders give up and return to their camp.

8. When does Coyote decide to help the humans get fire?
   - (A) after the Fire Holders scorch Coyote's tail
   - (B) in spring, after hundreds of humans are buried
   - (C) after he hears women weeping
   - (D) after the little boy human learns Coyote's language

9. Chipmunk's "badge of courage" is
   - (A) the three stripes down his back.
   - (B) his razor sharp fingers.
   - (C) a piece of wood with fire in it.
   - (D) a special pin that Coyote gave him after they stole fire from the Fire Holders.

10. Which of these is the best summary of the folktale?
    - (A) Three fierce Fire Holders keep the secret of fire from humans.
    - (B) Coyote makes a plan to help humans stay warm.
    - (C) Coyote and his friends steal fire from the Fire Holders and give it to humans.
    - (D) Coyote steals fire and is almost caught by one of the Fire Holders.

11. If the folktale continued, what do you think might happen next?

  (A) Humans will wage war against the Fire Holders.

  (B) Humans will learn to use fire to cook.

  (C) Coyote will steal fire from the humans.

  (D) The Fire Holders will never go into their tent again.

12. Which statement best expresses the main idea of the story?

  (A) Keeping secrets is a bad idea.

  (B) Fire is dangerous in the wrong hands.

  (C) Cooperation often leads to success.

  (D) Only the strong survive.

Extend Your Learning

- *Write a Folktale*

  The folktale you read answers a question about nature and the world we live in: How did humans get fire? Think of a similar question, such as "How did the stars get in the sky?" or "Why is the ocean salty?" Write your question and create a sequence chain to plan a series of events to tell your story. Follow your sequence chain to write your folktale. Draw a picture to show one important event of your folktale. Share your folktale by reading it aloud or including it in a classroom folktale anthology.

- *Play with a Folktale*

  Use the folktale "Coyote Brings Fire to Humans" or another folktale from an anthology, a book, or a magazine. Work with a group to rewrite the folktale as a play script. Cast the members of your group as characters, and present the folktale aloud to the class. You can add sets, props, and costumes to make your presentation more entertaining.

- *Sequence an Event*

  An interesting thing about sequence chains is that they frequently show not only the order in which events happen in time, but also how one event causes another event to happen, which causes another event to happen, and so on. Recall a meaningful event in your life. Then recall the events that led up to and that followed that special event. Create a sequence chain that shows the order of all these events. Examine your completed sequence chain to see how this one important moment is related to other events in your life.

STRATEGY FOUR · Recognizing Cause and Effect

Learn About Recognizing Cause and Effect

Thinking about the strategy

Everything you experience is a series of **causes and effects**. A cause is the reason something happens. An effect is what happens.

Cause: Your clock alarm goes off. —┌ Effect: You get up for school.
                                     └ Effect: You get to school on time.

Cause: You get to school on time. —— Effect: You are on time for classes.

Looking for causes and effects in a reading selection can be complicated because one cause can have many effects, and one effect can have many causes. Moreover, an effect can become a cause for the next event. In the example above, one effect of your clock alarm going off is that you get to school on time. Getting to school on time is also the cause of your being on time for classes, which is the effect.

When you read, look for the ways that an author uses causes and effects to link events and/or information. Authors sometimes signal causes and effects with words such as *since, because, this led to, so*, and *as a result*. In a narrative, or story, the causes and effects make up the events of the plot. In an essay, the causes and effects may be part of the information you need to read and understand.

Studying a model

Read the passage and the notes beside it.

The Right Stuff

The first cause is that the Montgolfier brothers decided to test their invention.

The test is the effect— they sent three animals for a balloon ride.

The continued work on balloons caused them to become more reliable.

The effect that balloons were more reliable is a cause that led to their use in warfare.

Clue words: As a result, so

Have you ever flown in a hot-air balloon? If you have, then you have something in common with a sheep, a rooster, and a duck. They were passengers on a Montgolfier brothers' hot-air balloon. In September of 1783, the brothers decided to launch the balloon to test the safety of their new invention. And eight minutes later, the animals set down alive and well. This successful flight led to a Montgolfier balloon flight carrying human passengers in November 1783.

As a result of the Montgolfiers' continued improvements and success and that of other balloonists, ballooning quickly became more reliable. So the technology found a wartime use. In France, in 1794, military personnel ascended in tethered balloons. From the height, they could survey the landscape and observe troop movements. It was not a sheepish place to roost, but they did not have to duck artillery fire!

34

Learn About a Graphic Organizer

*Understanding a
cause-effect diagram*
A **cause-effect diagram** helps you organize a reading selection into the important causes and effects. You can see how certain events, ideas, or facts are related to other information in the passage. You see that an effect often becomes a cause for the next event.

Look at this cause-effect diagram for the passage on page 34.

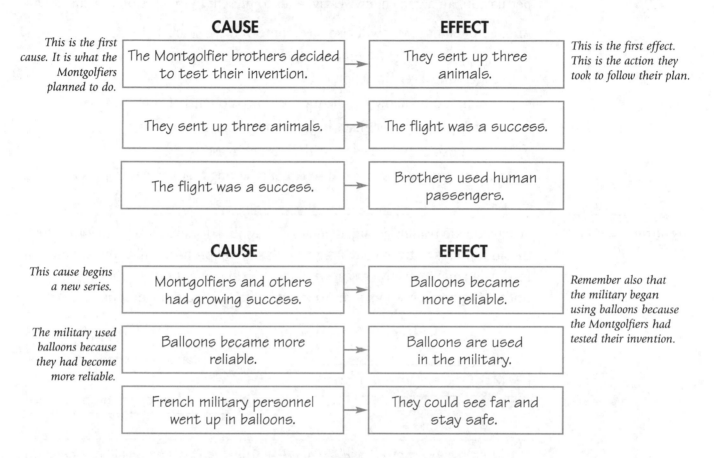

This is the first cause. It is what the Montgolfiers planned to do.

CAUSE

The Montgolfier brothers decided to test their invention.

They sent up three animals.

The flight was a success.

EFFECT

They sent up three animals.

This is the first effect. This is the action they took to follow their plan.

The flight was a success.

Brothers used human passengers.

This cause begins a new series.

The military used balloons because they had become more reliable.

CAUSE

Montgolfiers and others had growing success.

Balloons became more reliable.

French military personnel went up in balloons.

EFFECT

Balloons became more reliable.

Remember also that the military began using balloons because the Montgolfiers had tested their invention.

Balloons are used in the military.

They could see far and stay safe.

A cause-effect diagram helps you follow the author's thinking. You can better answer questions about the information.

What was the effect of the Montgolfiers using animals for their test flight?
They learned that animals would survive the flight, which led to using human passengers.

As you read, ask yourself

- What makes this happen, or what is the cause?
  What happens, or what is the effect?
- What clue words signal causes and effects?

Learn About a Form of Writing

Focusing on an argumentative essay

An **argumentative essay** is nonfiction that seeks to convince the reader of something. The simplest argument is a statement of what the author believes or feels (an opinion) supported by facts and reasons. By providing facts and information, along with clear and logical reasoning, the author tries to convince the reader to think the same way the author does on the topic. Unlike persuasion, an argumentative essay tends to present both sides of an issue.

An argumentative essay will also have some of these characteristics.

- The purpose may go beyond convincing the reader of some fact or opinion to suggesting a certain action.
- The main point, known as the proposition, is often stated in the essay.
- The proposition is one that can be debated—not a simple fact.
- The proposition is backed up with facts and reasons.
- An argumentative essay may also contain writing that appeals to the emotions.

Organizing ideas in a cause-effect diagram

When you are reading an argumentative essay, look for the causes and effects that the author uses to try to convince you of his or her proposition. Suppose you were reading an argumentative essay written by a sixth-grade student about whether or not to lengthen the school year. Your cause-effect diagram might look like this.

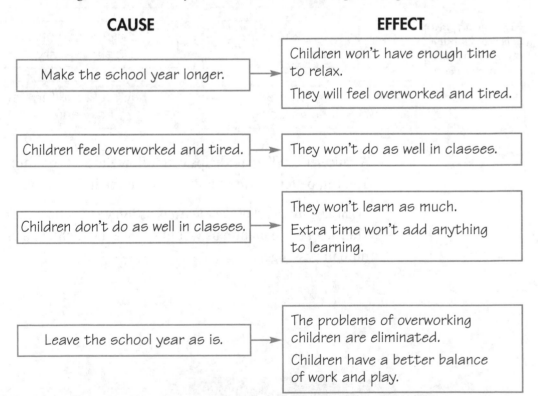

A cause-effect diagram goes through the argument step-by-step to help you see how sound the argument really is. Are the causes and effects accurate? Does each cause actually lead to the stated effect? Are the effects important?

Prepare for the Reading Selection

Gaining knowledge

Argumentative reading selections, including essays, speeches, and editorials, are used by people in different professions. Lawyers argue to persuade juries of the innocence of clients; journalists argue to convince people to change their beliefs or to persuade them to take action for a cause; politicians argue to affect laws and to gain votes; scientists argue to support theories. But not all arguments are the same.

Some arguments provide mostly facts and information to nudge the reader toward the desired conclusion. That an argument is taking place may not even be obvious at first. Other arguments are loaded with emotional words to make the reader react personally to the argument. They may use propaganda—devices that sway people's thinking, sometimes inappropriately. These types of arguments are persuasion, with the goal of getting the reader to move into action.

As you read the argumentative essay on the following pages, evaluate what type of argument is offered. You may be surprised by the author's final position on the topic!

Learn Vocabulary

Understanding vocabulary

The boxed words below are **boldfaced** in the selection. Learn the meaning of each word. Then complete the sentence with the correct word or term.

greenhouse effect
industrialization
global warming
dissipating
paleoclimatologists
sediment
cubic
variable

1. Factories, industries, and power plants are signs of _____ .

2. In a greenhouse, the sun's heat is trapped by the glass to keep the air warm; when this same type of thing happens with the atmosphere on the planet,

   scientists call it the _____ _____.

3. Scientists who study ancient climates are _____.

4. Some people believe the whole earth is growing warmer; they believe

   _____ _____ is a reality.

5. The volume of a cube can be measured in _____ inches.

6. In an experiment, the one thing you change, or vary, is called the

   _____ .

7. Since the clouds were _____, we could tell the storm had ended.

8. Studying the layers of rock, we could see which _____ had been laid down first.

Read the first part of the argumentative essay "Climate Change: Hotter? Colder? Wiser!"

Climate Change: Hotter? Colder? Wiser!

TODAY'S GREENHOUSE EFFECT

Everyone has heard about the **greenhouse effect**. The sun's heat gets trapped by certain gases in the atmosphere. As a result, Earth gets warmer. The greenhouse gases include carbon dioxide, methane, water vapor, and ozone. Some scientists say that **industrialization**, including the burning of fossil fuels (coal, oil, and natural gas), has increased the concentration of greenhouse gases found in the lower atmosphere. These greenhouse gases, along with particles such as cloud droplets, soot, and dust, contribute to a spiraling process that traps more and more heat close to the surface. As the heat in the lower atmosphere builds, the surface of Earth becomes warmer. These scientists therefore state that industrialization has contributed to—or even created— measurable human-made **global warming**. But this statement leads me to ask two questions: Is the greenhouse effect only caused by industrialization? Is global warming really taking place?

GREENHOUSE EFFECT OF THE PAST

The greenhouse effect is not new. In fact, this effect began long before humans existed on the planet. It is one of the factors that provide, with the sun's help, a liveable Earth temperature.

Heat from the sun reaches the blanket of atmosphere surrounding the planet. A little less than one third of the energy from the sun is immediately reflected back into space; a little less than one third is absorbed by the atmosphere. The remaining third reaches the surface. Some of this energy reflects back and warms the lower atmosphere. Some heats the lands and the waters, which in turn also heat the air above them. The layers of atmosphere with their greenhouse gases keep the reflected heat from **dissipating** outward into space. Earth stays warm. So I can conclude that the greenhouse effect is not all bad nor solely caused by humans.

STUDYING THE PAST

So, how can we tell if Earth's still growing industrialization has increased the greenhouse effect to produce significant global warming? To answer this question, a new breed of scientists, **paleoclimatologists**, look to the past for answers about the present. They study variations in Earth's climate of the past.

Warmer temperatures hold more carbon dioxide in the air, which in turn produces more carbon in tree rings. So paleoclimatologists look at changes in tree rings. These scientists also analyze ancient ice. Cores of ice drilled from Antarctica show climate variations over the past 160,000 years. They also study the chemical makeup of ocean **sediment** layers.

Not surprisingly, all three sources reveal heating up and cooling of the climate, an effect caused most likely by changes in the sun and by the effects of volcanoes. But these natural variations do not necessarily explain the apparent large increase in temperature since the mid-1800s, the start of the Industrial Age. So could this be just the human-made greenhouse effect warming up the globe?

Completing a cause-effect diagram

Fill in the cause-effect diagrams for the sections TODAY'S GREENHOUSE EFFECT and GREENHOUSE EFFECT OF THE PAST. (You may need to add more details to some of the effects.) Create a cause-effect diagram for the causes and effects in STUDYING THE PAST on a separate piece of paper.

TODAY'S GREENHOUSE EFFECT

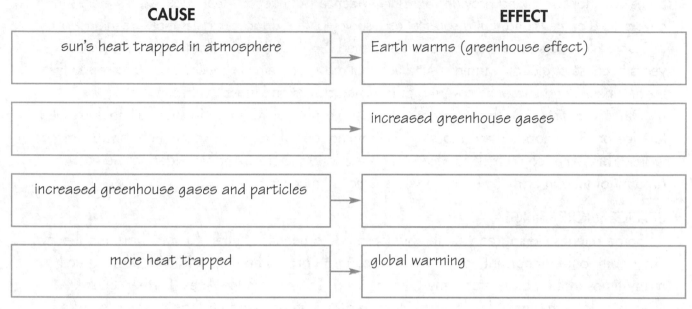

CAUSE	EFFECT
sun's heat trapped in atmosphere	Earth warms (greenhouse effect)
	increased greenhouse gases
increased greenhouse gases and particles	
more heat trapped	global warming

GREENHOUSE EFFECT OF THE PAST

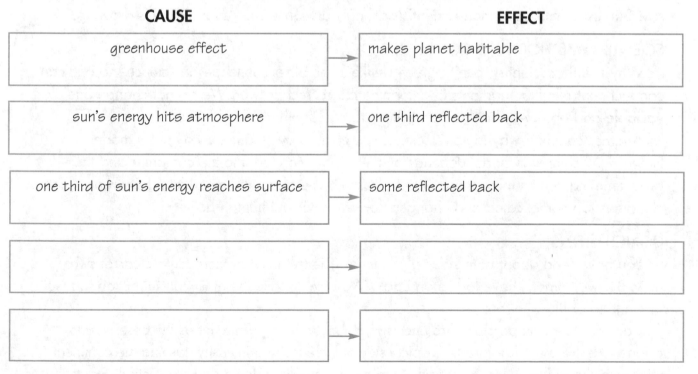

CAUSE	EFFECT
greenhouse effect	makes planet habitable
sun's energy hits atmosphere	one third reflected back
one third of sun's energy reaches surface	some reflected back

Read the second part of the argumentative essay "Climate Change: Hotter? Colder? Wiser!"

SEA ICE DIMINISHING!

Some scientists cite diminishing sea ice and shrinking glaciers as proof of global warming. Some say that Greenland provides absolute evidence. A huge ice sheet about 1,500 meters thick covers 85% of the island. But a satellite laser survey of the surface suggests that Greenland lost 51 **cubic** kilometers of sea ice, out of an estimated 2,600,000 cubic kilometers, in the past 5 years because of global warming. Although that may not seem like much, it could raise sea level by 6.4 meters and cause the covering of low-lying shores and islands with seawater.

Other scientists view this differently. They say a natural variation in snowfall could result in less ice on Greenland. They also suggest that changes in ocean currents might bring warmer water. This water could melt sea ice along the island's shores. And considering the vast amount of time in Earth's history, 5 years is not significant.

SEA ICE INCREASING!

Some scientists disagree with the human-made greenhouse effect/global warming theory. They point out that normal variations have caused Earth to heat up and cool down greatly many times in the past, before any humans lived. Think of the Ice Ages. Further, these scientists claim the air of the lower atmosphere isn't greatly warmer than it was a hundred years ago. They suggest it is cooler. This cooler temperature caused sea ice around parts of Antarctica to grow over the past 20 years. "A little more significant than 5 years," they say. But just a little. And many scientists strongly disagree that Antarctic ice is growing.

SCIENTIFIC METHOD AND COMPUTERS

Why is it that scientists can't agree? Unlike some other challenges in science, no one can conduct controlled experiments to determine the correct answer. We cannot change one **variable** and observe what happens, then change another and observe.

Another common way to solve science questions is by creating a computer model. However, a computer model depends on the information fed into the computer and the programming, which may or may not be correct. Therefore, the model can be wrong. Earth's climate is too complicated and changeable—even without human activity.

CONCLUSIONS

You have read about both sides of the issue. The truth is that there is no clear answer now. But we humans have to live on Earth. We have to take the most careful action to result in the kind of life we want.

Consider these six possible dire effects of global warming. Rain floods the deserts, and aridness destroys the rainforests. Tropical storms increase and intensify, lashing the continents with record-breaking winds and rain—and record-breaking death and destruction. Plants that have evolved for eons wither or die because of sudden changes. Animal species face a similar cruel fate. Melting ice causes a rise in sea level, burying coastal cities in seawater.

We can limit the use of fossil fuels to help prevent these catastrophes. We can control pollution with laws and responsible choices. We can, and must, create long-range pollution-free energy sources. Then, on a cleaner, better Earth, we can wait for the next accepted climate theory—or the next one hundred or more years or centuries to pass.

Using a cause-effect diagram

Use the cause-effect diagrams to help organize the information in the second part of the argumentative essay. Diagram the causes and effects in the CONCLUSIONS section on a separate piece of paper.

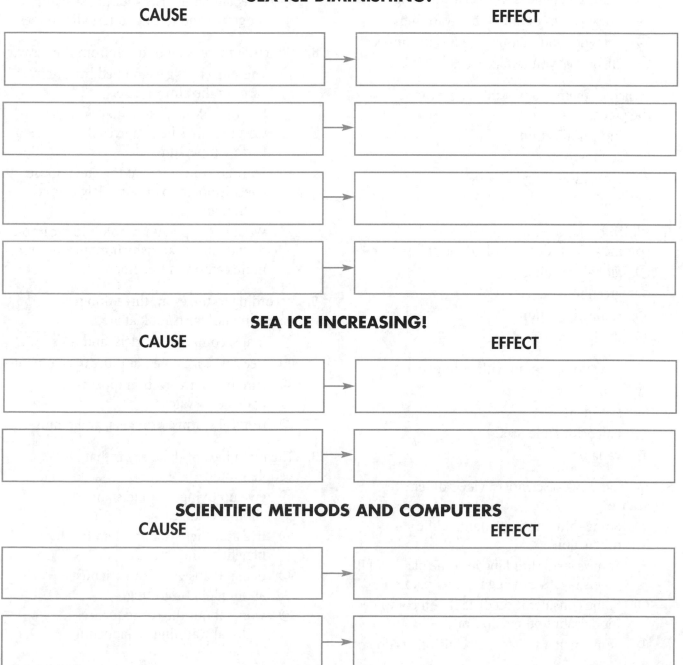

SEA ICE DIMINISHING!

CAUSE	EFFECT

SEA ICE INCREASING!

CAUSE	EFFECT

SCIENTIFIC METHODS AND COMPUTERS

CAUSE	EFFECT

Check Your Understanding

Think about what you've read. Then answer these questions.

1. Which of these is cited as a cause of global warming?
   - Ⓐ diminishing sea ice
   - Ⓑ increased industrialization
   - Ⓒ tropical storms
   - Ⓓ computer models

2. What effect did the author hope to achieve by showing you the conflicting scientific beliefs?
   - Ⓐ make you believe in global warming
   - Ⓑ cause you to doubt global warming
   - Ⓒ convince you that no one has the answer
   - Ⓓ encourage you to take sides

3. Which of these is a possible effect of the greenhouse effect?
   - Ⓐ industrialization
   - Ⓑ sediment
   - Ⓒ global warming
   - Ⓓ cubic

4. Which of these means "the increased commercial production of goods and services"?
   - Ⓐ global warming
   - Ⓑ greenhouse effect
   - Ⓒ industrialization
   - Ⓓ dissipating

5. Which word has to do with volume?
   - Ⓐ cubic
   - Ⓑ sediment
   - Ⓒ paleoclimatologists
   - Ⓓ variable

6. In what way do scientists' views differ over sea ice?
   - Ⓐ Some think it's important, while others don't.
   - Ⓑ Some say it's shrinking in some places, while others say it's growing in other places.
   - Ⓒ Some consider it predictable on computer models, but others do not.
   - Ⓓ Some melt it for testing, while others do not.

7. Complete this summary of the essay by choosing the best ending: The author believes that since scientists can't agree on or predict global warming,
   - Ⓐ we should all live the way we want.
   - Ⓑ they better get busy and find the answer before it's too late.
   - Ⓒ people should take reasonable action to limit the possible consequences.
   - Ⓓ paleoclimatologists should use computer programs and testing to test all theories.

8. Which of these is an opinion from the essay?
   - Ⓐ The sun's heat gets trapped by certain gases in the atmosphere.
   - Ⓑ It is one of the factors that provide, with the sun's help, a liveable Earth temperature.
   - Ⓒ So I can conclude that the greenhouse effect is not all bad nor solely caused by humans.
   - Ⓓ Warmer temperatures hold more carbon dioxide in the air, which in turn produces more carbon in tree rings.

9. According to the essay, three things paleoclimatologists look at are
   - Ⓐ maps, computer models, and tests.
   - Ⓑ tree rings, ice cores, and ocean sediment.
   - Ⓒ current sea ice, carbon dioxide, and ocean water.
   - Ⓓ tropical storms, droughts, and plants.

10. The main idea of the essay is that people should
   - Ⓐ give up trying to understand climate change.
   - Ⓑ live as if there is a problem for the benefit of the future.
   - Ⓒ demand answers from scientists about global warming.
   - Ⓓ worry about the consequences if global warming is happening.

11. What happens right after one third of the sun's energy reaches the surface?

- Ⓐ One third reflects back into space from the upper atmosphere.
- Ⓑ One third is absorbed by the atmosphere.
- Ⓒ Part reflects off the surface, and part heats land and water.
- Ⓓ Earth heats up.

12. Fossil fuels are

- Ⓐ carbon dioxide, methane, water vapor, and ozone.
- Ⓑ coal, oil, and natural gas.
- Ⓒ cloud droplets, soot, and dust.
- Ⓓ carbon dioxide, coal, and oil.

Extend Your Learning

- *Learn More About the Greenhouse Effect*

  Research to find an article about the greenhouse effect and global warming in a textbook, a magazine, a newspaper, or on the web. Read the article and create a cause-effect diagram for the article. Then compare it to this argumentative essay. Does your article support one side of the issue presented in this essay or the other? How do you know?

- *Create a Model*

  Work with a group to create a model that demonstrates the greenhouse effect and/or global warming. Present your model to the class. Explain what your model shows.

- *Write an Argument*

  Plan and write an argumentative essay about something important to you. You can use any topic that can be debated, such as why school sports are important for everyone, why dogs make better pets than cats, why space exploration budgets should be cut, or why homework should be eliminated. You can use just facts and sound reasoning in your argument, or you can add emotional words and propaganda. Read your argumentative essay to some classmates for their response.

Comparing and Contrasting

Learn About Comparing and Contrasting

Thinking about the strategy

Authors often describe two or more people, places, events, ideas, or objects. One way they present the important details about two or more people or things is by **comparing and contrasting**. When you compare, you consider how things are alike. Clue words such as *both, all, similar, like,* and *in common* signal comparisons. When you contrast, you consider how things are different. Clue words such as *in contrast, however, but, unlike, different,* and *on the other hand* signal contrasts. Often, the author gives no clue words. Then you need to look for the comparisons and contrasts.

Comparing and contrasting help you clearly picture what is being described so that you can draw your own conclusions about the people, places, or things.

Studying a model

Read the passage and the notes beside it.

The Race

In the first paragraph, you learn how Marcos and Jake are alike and different in appearance and behavior at the starting line.

The boys waited at the starting line. Marcos bounced around, looking lean but wild in shiny green silk shorts and a white muscle T-shirt. His brown hair flipped over his eyebrows, almost covering his lashes. He kept shaking his arms and hands, and dancing around nervously. Jake stood next to him, calm, confident, and serious in plain black shorts and white T-shirt. His cropped hair lay perfectly neat. You could see by the way his arms hung at his sides and his stance stayed relaxed that he hadn't a hint of tension.

In the second paragraph, you see the differences in the way they race, along with the similarities: for example, they are both determined to win.

Clue words: also, but, both

The starter's pistol sounded. Determined to win, Marcos bounded off without hesitation in a pinwheel whirl of limbs. He pounded hard to pull ahead of the pack. Jake, planning on first place, also left the block instantly. But with his huge gliding strides, he looked as if he were rowing through the air, evenly gaining speed. Marcos glanced anxiously behind and whirred off again, limbs aflutter, to run faster. He gained distance yet with Jake's steady acceleration and easy grace, the distance could easily vanish. Both boys breathed deep and hard.

Learn About a Graphic Organizer

A **Venn diagram** makes comparing and contrasting easy. You may learn that two characters who seem very similar have a striking difference. You may find that two settings have something in common that you did not notice at first.

Look at this Venn diagram for the first paragraph of the passage on page 44. It displays the comparison between Marcos and Jake.

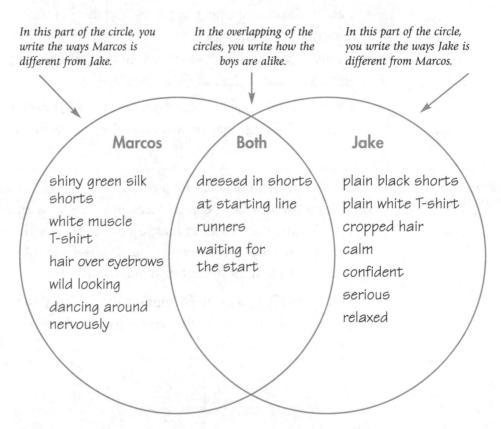

In this part of the circle, you write the ways Marcos is different from Jake.

In the overlapping of the circles, you write how the boys are alike.

In this part of the circle, you write the ways Jake is different from Marcos.

Marcos

shiny green silk shorts

white muscle T-shirt

hair over eyebrows

wild looking

dancing around nervously

Both

dressed in shorts

at starting line

runners

waiting for the start

Jake

plain black shorts

plain white T-shirt

cropped hair

calm

confident

serious

relaxed

A Venn diagram helps you see how the characters are alike and different. You can better understand how they think, react, and behave. You can draw conclusions and make predictions more easily.

How do you think the two boys will compare when they run?
Marcos may be flashier yet more nervous; Jake may be smoother, stronger, and calmer.

As you read, ask yourself

- How are the people, places, objects, events, and ideas alike and different?
- Does the author signal similarities and differences with words such as *alike, unlike, similar, different*?

Learn About a Form of Writing

Focusing on a descriptive essay

A **descriptive essay** is one in which the author describes people, places, or things in great detail. Descriptive writing often forms part of a narrative or an argument. Yet it can also stand alone.

A descriptive essay has the following characteristics.

- A descriptive essay may be fiction or nonfiction.
- Details that describe people, places, and things are the most important elements.
- Events and actions are used to tell more about the people, places, and things rather than to tell a story.
- The description makes use of figurative language and imagery.
- A descriptive essay may be written in the first person, *I*.

Organizing ideas in a Venn diagram

You can use a Venn diagram for a descriptive essay whenever the author is presenting two or more people, places, or things. A Venn diagram lays out the similarities and differences so that you can clearly see the ways the people, places, and things are alike and different. You also have the information you need to form opinions and make your own judgments.

"The Race" on page 44 is the beginning of an essay describing Marcos and Jake. Study the Venn diagram for the second paragraph, which compares the way the two runners start the race.

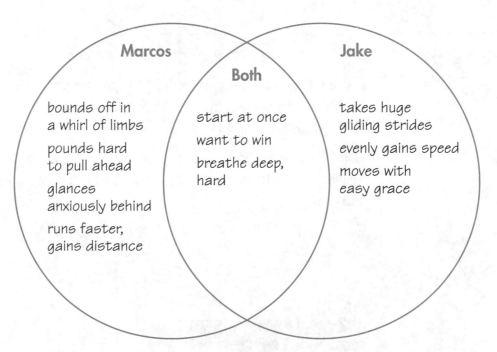

Marcos

bounds off in a whirl of limbs

pounds hard to pull ahead

glances anxiously behind

runs faster, gains distance

Both

start at once

want to win

breathe deep, hard

Jake

takes huge gliding strides

evenly gains speed

moves with easy grace

Prepare for the Reading Selection

Gaining knowledge

A character sketch is one kind of description that can stand alone as an essay or be part of a narrative. In a character sketch, the author uses many details to describe characters. The author may focus on physical appearance, such as facial features or body type or clothing. The author may present the character's personality through decisions the character makes, such as choices of friends, hobbies, interests, and sports. Behaviors and habits reveal how the character feels about himself/herself and others. Sometimes, family background and living conditions add to the description. The author may tell you about the character directly, provide information through detailed actions and events, and/or include dialogue in which the character reveals thoughts, attitudes, and feelings.

To create a good character sketch, the author uses descriptive words and strong verbs. Much of the language appeals to the senses—sight, hearing, taste, sound, and/or touch. Precise details reveal the type of person the character is. Clear and strong images allow the reader to experience the character. On the following pages, you will read a descriptive essay about two girls.

Learn Vocabulary

Understanding vocabulary

The boxed words below are **boldfaced** in the selection. Learn the meaning of each word. Then write the word that completes the sentence.

managerial
paternal
self-effacing
mansion
saguaros
stucco
rough-hewn
mucky
canopy
gauzy
honeysuckle

1. She was so _____ you could easily overlook her presence.

2. The _____ in the garden smelled sweet.

3. Rather than being sanded smooth, the wood was _____.

4. The shallow water was dark and _____.

5. Like a huge umbrella, the _____ shaded the lawn.

6. The cloth was not firmly woven but was fragile and _____.

7. The _____ consisted of cement, red sand, and lime.

8. Maternal, "of the mother," is the opposite of _____, "of the father."

9. The huge cactuses with upward-curving branches are _____.

10. The _____ had been built by a millionaire for his family.

11. He took charge of the business when he gained the _____ position.

Read the first part of the descriptive essay "I'd Like to Introduce Maria. . . ."

I'd Like to Introduce Maria . . .

I'd like to introduce you to Maria—actually to two girls named Maria. One is Maria Rosalita Gonzales, my cousin from Arizona—and the best friend a girl could ever have. The other is my friend Maria Johnson, who lives in a rural town near Worcester, Massachusetts.

Maria Rosalita Gonzales was born in a city in Colombia, South America. She came to the United States when she was five years old. Her father Julio had acquired a **managerial** position in Phoenix, Arizona. So the whole family, Maria and her three sisters and two brothers, moved to the suburbs of Phoenix. If they hadn't moved to the states, I might never have had a chance to become her good friend. You see, my mother is a sister of Maria's father. My mother met and married my dad, a Swede named Jorgensson, when he visited Colombia in the 1970s. They moved to New York City, where we now live in an apartment.

The family calls Maria Rosalita by the name Marirosa. Uncle Julio started the nickname as "Marirosa la Mariposa." You see, in Spanish, *mariposa* is butterfly, and Marirosa is as beautiful and delicate and flighty as a butterfly. She has gleaming long black hair. When she turns her head, her hair flares out, catching the sun's rays on every shiny shaft. And Maria frequently shakes her head because she knows how lovely this looks. Her large eyes are deep brown with golden streaks and flecks. Her skin is light russet.

Marirosa is 4 feet 11 inches tall, and she is 11 years old. Her clothes make her a rainbow, as she chooses a range of bright colors to layer in unique T-shirts and jerseys and sweaters and leggings. Her shoes are never plain, but some incredible bright color—turquoise flats or lime green low heels. Even her sneakers are bright pink or salmon red, not white.

Now, my friend Maria Johnson is very different from Marirosa. Maria's **paternal** grandparents moved to Massachusetts from Sweden in the early 1930s. At first, her grandfather Johnson worked on a farm. When he had saved enough, he and his wife Elise bought the farm. It was hard work, but they did well and raised corn and dairy cows and a family of four. Maria's dad Peter was their oldest child. He married a Finnish girl, Mary Ellen Kahkola, and when Peter's parents died, Maria's parents ran the farm for awhile. So when Maria was little, she played with the kittens in the barn and wandered the fields, looking for wild juicy raspberries in summer and soft pussy willows in spring.

Maria has short blond hair that glows copper in the sun. Her hazel eyes dance with joy when she looks at anything in nature. She is 11 years old and 4 feet 8 inches tall—that's moderately tall, at least taller than I am. Her skin is not white as snow, but it is clear and bright. When she gets cold or angry, her cheeks blush bright pink—a striking contrast to her fair skin.

One thing I like about Maria is the way she dresses. You never see her in a plain T-shirt or jeans, but always in soft blouses and skirts that make her look like a gypsy. Her earrings—her ears are pierced and she always wears earrings—are long chains or hoops of gold or silver. Yet never do I feel as if Maria thinks about how she looks—she's not **self-effacing** but she's not even a bit conceited. I can imagine Maria dancing around a gypsy wagon, her skirts swishing and rustling like wind-blown leaves. And the colors she wears are like leaves too—bright green summer leaves and red and gold and yellow autumn leaves.

Completing a Venn diagram

Some of the Venn diagram for the first part of the descriptive essay has been filled in. Add more details to compare and contrast the two girls.

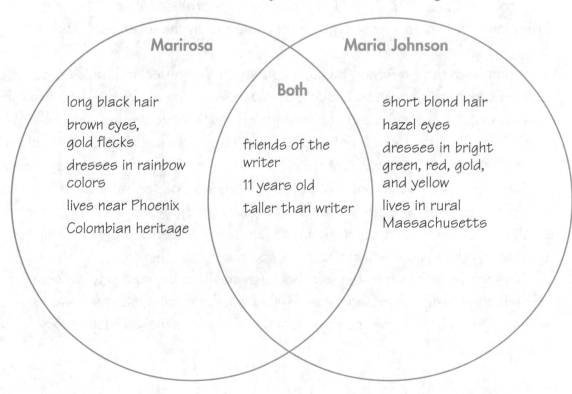

Marirosa

long black hair

brown eyes, gold flecks

dresses in rainbow colors

lives near Phoenix

Colombian heritage

Both

friends of the writer

11 years old

taller than writer

Maria Johnson

short blond hair

hazel eyes

dresses in bright green, red, gold, and yellow

lives in rural Massachusetts

Read the second part of the descriptive essay "I'd Like to Introduce Maria. . . ."

Early last summer Dad and I flew to Phoenix. Uncle Julio and Marirosa met us at the airport and we drove to Marirosa's new house—a **mansion**, I would call it. The first thing I saw was the huge fence wrapping around the whole complex. Cottonwoods grew in the river valley, but near the fence were tall **saguaros**—with tiny holes where burrowing owls live— and a lot of sagebrush. Marirosa jumped lightly out of the car and fluttered to the black iron gate and swung it open. We drove through. Then she flitted back into the car, and we progressed up the long driveway to the house.

Aunt Rosa greeted us at a reddish stone arch, and we entered a stone patio. Some of the rooms, all with red **stucco** outer walls and large sliding doors, opened onto this patio, which overflowed with colorful flowers and vines. A whirring buzz that lifted my hair was the first hummingbird I had ever felt! Many of these jewel-like birds darted from flower to flower as we strolled toward the main door.

Once inside, Marirosa showed me her room. One door opened to the patio and one to an inner courtyard with a small, deep turquoise pool! We both changed into suits—of course, Marirosa's was more colorful than mine—and we swam in the warm but refreshing water.

Later in the day, Marirosa gave me a tour of the house. All the rooms (including ten bedrooms!) had simple yet beautiful furniture, fantastic views, and white plastered walls— very cool and pleasing. A few large paintings decorated hallways, but mostly there were lush plants and colorful flowers. I felt fortunate to stay the week with Marirosa and her family while Dad worked.

When Dad and I returned home, we flew into Worcester and rented a car to drive to Maria Johnson's house so I could spend two weeks there. Maria's house is a farmhouse, even though her family doesn't farm anymore. It sits on about five acres of farmland—mostly fields with a bordering forest of maples, oaks, and scattered pines. The circular driveway curves just at the large oak front door, the most elaborate part of the gray wooden house.

The farmhouse has an entryway of **rough-hewn** wood, an arbor, that leads into what is called a mudroom because you enter with your muddy shoes. The inner door opens to a small hallway with stairs going up to the four second-floor bedrooms. On the main floor, an eat-in kitchen is on the right and a living room is on the left.

I took my suitcase up to Maria's room, which sits in the northwest corner of the house. Her windows overlook the backyard, with a small natural pond where we used to swim when we were little. Now, the three-foot depth of water makes it too **mucky** for us.

Maria's bed is huge and fancy, with a **canopy** and **gauzy** curtains. I feel like a princess sleeping in that bed! She also has a huge puffy chair. Her wallpaper is bright yellow with tulips.

As soon as I dropped off my suitcase, Maria led me to her summer garden. She said if we stayed quiet amid the trumpet vines and **honeysuckle**, we would see a hummingbird. I did not tell her that I had seen hundreds of hummingbirds, all different glistening colors, at my cousin's. Sure enough, a little ruby-throated appeared and whizzed to a glass feeder Maria had hung amid the blooms.

"Amazing, aren't they? How exquisite and different they are from all the other birds! Yet all the birds are beautiful, don't you think, Anna?" Maria asked.

I smiled in agreement, but mostly I was thinking about my two friends—how exquisite and different and beautiful they are.

Using a Venn diagram

In the second part of the essay, the author describes the girls' homes. Fill in the Venn Diagram with details that compare and contrast where the two Marias live.

_____   _____

Both

Check Your Understanding

Think about what you've read. Then answer these questions.

1. What is one way that Maria Rosalita Gonzales (Marirosa) and Maria Johnson are alike?
   - Ⓐ They both are shorter than the writer.
   - Ⓑ They both have dark hair.
   - Ⓒ They both were born in the United States.
   - Ⓓ They both dress to please themselves.

2. What is one way Marirosa is different from Maria Johnson?
   - Ⓐ Marirosa loves to swim but Maria has never swum.
   - Ⓑ Marirosa can seem slightly conceited but Maria never tries to impress people.
   - Ⓒ Marirosa lives with her parents but Maria lives with her grandparents on a farm.
   - Ⓓ Marirosa is interested in birds but Maria is not.

3. Mucky water would most likely be found in a
   - Ⓐ swimming pool.
   - Ⓑ deep ocean.
   - Ⓒ shallow pond.
   - Ⓓ rapidly flowing stony river.

4. Which word completes the analogy?
   manager:managerial::father:_____
   - Ⓐ canopy
   - Ⓒ saguaros
   - Ⓑ self-effacing
   - Ⓓ paternal

5. A stucco house would look most like a
   - Ⓐ log cabin.
   - Ⓑ rough-hewn wood cottage.
   - Ⓒ home built of cemented field stones.
   - Ⓓ home covered with plaster.

6. In the second paragraph on page 51, the author states "a little ruby-throated appeared." What is the author referring to?
   - Ⓐ a younger sister with a red scarf
   - Ⓑ a flowering plant
   - Ⓒ a hummingbird
   - Ⓓ a small red-necked gecko

7. The author's main purpose is to
   - Ⓐ tell a story about meeting her two friends.
   - Ⓑ persuade you to like her two friends as much as she does.
   - Ⓒ explain the facts about life in rural Massachusetts and Phoenix, Arizona.
   - Ⓓ help you picture her two friends in great detail.

8. The use of the word *fluttered* in the first paragraph on page 50 reminds the reader that Marirosa
   - Ⓐ is like a butterfly.
   - Ⓑ is awkward in her movements.
   - Ⓒ makes a lot of noise when she moves.
   - Ⓓ jumps about a lot.

9. What does the author reveal about herself when she does not tell Maria Johnson about the hundreds of hummingbirds she saw in Phoenix?
   - Ⓐ She obviously doesn't like Maria Johnson enough to share her experiences with her.
   - Ⓑ She cares enough for her friend that she does not want to spoil the joy of seeing Maria's single hummingbird.
   - Ⓒ She is jealous of both her friends' beautiful homes and gardens since she lives in a New York City apartment.
   - Ⓓ She is selfish about her other friend and won't even let Maria Johnson know that she has another friend.

10. What can you definitely tell about the size of Marirosa's bedroom?
    - Ⓐ It extends from the front of the house to an inner courtyard.
    - Ⓑ It takes up one tenth of the house.
    - Ⓒ It sits in one corner of the house.
    - Ⓓ It is larger than Maria Johnson's bedroom.

11. Which sentence from the descriptive essay is an opinion?

Ⓐ If they hadn't moved to the states, I might never have had a chance to become her good friend.

Ⓑ As soon as I dropped off my suitcase, Maria led me to her summer garden.

Ⓒ Marirosa is 4 feet 11 inches tall, and she is 11 years old.

Ⓓ Her earrings—her ears are pierced and she always wears earrings—are long chains or hoops of gold or silver.

12. Which sentence is the best summary of the essay?

Ⓐ A girl describes the family background of her cousin and best friend.

Ⓑ A girl has two friends who appear very alike but live in different types of homes.

Ⓒ Three friends get together every summer to review their friendship.

Ⓓ A girl describes her two wonderful friends and their homes.

Extend Your Learning

- *Make your Own "Friend Venn"*

  Create a Venn diagram to compare the qualities of two of your friends, cousins, other relatives, or even pets. Think carefully about which qualities the people or pets share and which are unique. When you have finished, consider why you like these people or animals, even though they have differences.

- *Write Descriptions*

  Work in groups to create a detailed and effective description of a person, place, or thing. First create lists of details that will add to the description. Try to include words that appeal to the senses of sight, sound, touch, taste, and smell. Then work the details into a single effective essay for your group. Create one or more pictures to go with your description. Then share your work with another group.

- *Describe an Object*

  Choose a common object and write a short descriptive paragraph about the object. You might tell what it looks like, feels like, smells like, tastes like, sounds like—but do not tell what it is. You can also describe how it is used or how people react to it, or any other description that would help people picture what the object is. Then work in groups, reading the descriptions and guessing the objects that are described.

Making Predictions

Learn About Making Predictions

Thinking about the strategy

When you hear or read a story, you often **make predictions** about what will happen next. *To predict* means "to guess in advance." Your guess is not a wild one, but one based on the facts, details, and events in the story combined with what you know from your own experience.

Imagine a friend calls. She says snowboarding classes start Tuesday and she's really interested in learning. She adds that her parents have given their permission. She doesn't tell you, but you predict she will be at the first snowboarding class.

| Snowboarding classes start Tuesday. | → | A friend is interested in learning. | → | The friend's parents approve. | → | The friend will be at class on Tuesday. |

In this example, you take what your friend tells you and what you know about her to make a logical prediction. This is similar to what you do when you read a story and predict what will happen next. Of course, your prediction may be right or wrong. You read on to check your prediction and make new ones.

Studying a model

Read the first part of the story and the notes beside it.

Into the Deep

Notice what is happening in the story.

Consider what you already know about the things you're reading about.

Pay attention to what Rebecca says and does.

What will Rebecca do about the heavy tank?

José, our instructor, told us to get our gear and climb aboard the small power boat that bounced and rocked on the choppy waters. I picked up the plastic carryall that held my snorkel, goggles, and fins. Then with my left arm, I awkwardly hoisted my heavy scuba tank. "How I will carry this on my back underwater, I do not know," I thought to myself. Then I remembered that the buoyancy of the water will make it feel less weighty.

"Put that here, Rebecca," José ordered, expecting me to lift the tank over the side of the boat, which suddenly looked awfully high. Well, I was here to learn how to do this myself.

Learn About a Graphic Organizer

Understanding a plot-line prediction diagram

A **plot-line prediction diagram** includes a step-by-step summary of the series of events, the plot, in a story, followed by your prediction of what will happen next. You can use a plot-line prediction diagram whenever you are reading, listening to, or watching a narrative to help you understand the plot and guess at outcomes.

Here is a plot-line prediction diagram for the story beginning on page 54. In note form, it includes the important events that lead up to the prediction.

You begin with the first important event in the plot and continue listing events in order as far as you have read.

> José tells Rebecca to get her gear and climb aboard.

> Rebecca picks up the equipment and scuba tank.

> José tells Rebecca to put the tank in the boat.

> Rebecca feels the tank is too heavy.

> Rebecca reminds herself she is here to learn.

Your prediction is based on the events in the plot.

PREDICTION

> Rebecca will manage to get the tank in the boat.

In a plot-line prediction diagram, you can clearly see the events in the plot and how the events relate to one another. Then you can make a prediction that is likely to be well-founded and accurate.

What is Rebecca here to do?
She is here to learn how to scuba dive.

As you read, ask yourself

- What is each event in the plot?
- Where is this series of events likely to lead?
- What clues does the author provide about what will happen next?
- What do I know about situations like this?

Learn About a Form of Writing

Focusing on a short story

A **short story** is a narrative. It is usually much shorter than a novel. A short story is a blend of characters, setting, plot, and theme. In one or more settings (places and times), the characters experience events and feelings that move the plot (series of events) forward. Through the events, actions, and outcomes, the theme (author's idea about life) is revealed.

These characteristics can help you recognize a short story.

- The narrative can be read in a single sitting.
- The plot is constructed with a beginning, a middle, and an end.
- Characters reveal themselves by action and dialogue.
- The theme ties the story together.
- A short story is fiction, though it may be based on real experiences.

Organizing ideas in a plot-line prediction diagram

On page 54, you read the beginning of a short story. Read the next part of the story and study the plot-line prediction diagram.

> On the bay, the water churned and swirled. Our little boat with its four students and instructor rocked mercilessly. I felt unnerved.
>
> "This is where we'll anchor and go over!" José announced. He threw out the anchor.
>
> "Okay, time to gear up. Put the regulator in your mouth, hold onto it with one hand, sit on the boat's side—two people on each side, please!—and fall backward exactly when I say," José barked.
>
> "Fall backward!" I screeched. I had never done that! I was terrified. Yet, José just stared blankly at me. I wanted to escape. But I was here for the experience, wasn't I?

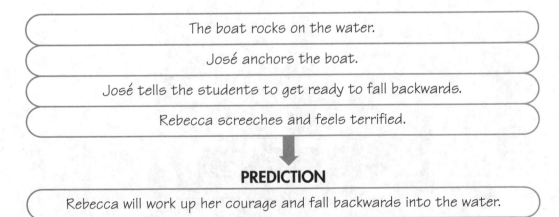

The boat rocks on the water.

José anchors the boat.

José tells the students to get ready to fall backwards.

Rebecca screeches and feels terrified.

PREDICTION

Rebecca will work up her courage and fall backwards into the water.

A plot-line prediction diagram, which shows how the plot leads step-by-step to the next logical outcome, helps you predict more accurately.

Prepare for the Reading Selection

Gaining knowledge

Short narratives have existed since people first told stories—stories about how to survive, where to find game, what happened during the hunt. But the modern short story is a narrative artform that emerged in the 19th century. As an artform, certain "rules" dictated the structure. The short story had to have developed characters, clear and detailed settings, and a well-constructed plot. It had to teach or suggest a lesson about life. The lesson is called the theme.

A short story often centers around a basic conflict. A person struggles against forces of nature, against another person, against society, or among conflicting parts of his or her inner nature. The conflict dictates the plot, but how it is resolved in the short story indicates the theme. In the short story you are about to read, think about where the major conflict lies. What does the main character know that helps him solve the conflict?

Learn Vocabulary

Understanding vocabulary

The boxed words below are **boldfaced** in the selection. Learn the meaning of each word. Then write the word that answers the question.

carnelian
polyurethane
efficiency
flotation
dilapidated
azure
plumage
momentum
absent-mindedly
tedious
queried

1. Which names a force that drives you forward? _____

2. Which is a synonym of *effectiveness*? _____

3. Which is something only a bird has? _____

4. Which is a stone that is pale to dark red? _____

5. Which could be used to describe the ocean? _____

6. Which is a synonym of *asked*? _____

7. Which is an antonym of *new*? _____

8. Which describes something that is boring? _____

9. Which means acting "without full attention"? _____

10. Which can protect and coat wood? _____

11. Which can help name a water-safety device? _____

Read the first part of the short story "Ripples on Lake Juniper."

Ripples on Lake Juniper

The sun rose in a blaze of gold and **carnelian** that was echoed on the still surface of Lake Juniper. In the cabin, Rusty Morgan yawned, stretched, crawled out of bed, and dressed. He then called to his son Marcus who was in the other tiny bedroom.

"Wake up, Marcus. A fantastic day is beginning, and we don't want to miss a minute of it." Rusty headed for the bathroom to wash up and get ready to make a fine vacation breakfast. He didn't wait to hear his son answer.

"Dad," Marcus yelled excitedly, pulling a T-shirt on as he stumbled out of his bedroom. "Is the weather okay for canoeing today? Are we really going to go?"

"Open your eyes and look out the window," Rusty urged, smiling at his twelve-year-old.

"Wow! It's fantastic. The water is so still. It's awesome!" Marcus exclaimed.

"Yes, it is calm and quiet now. I've noticed that there is always a time just after sunrise and sunset when the water here is perfectly still. Yet today the sky is cloudless. I'll check the weather forecast on the laptop and if it's good, we can plan to spend the day canoeing to Knoll Island and around the whole lake. We'll bring a picnic and lots of water. Sound good?" Rusty booted the computer and entered the weather address. "Mmm, fine prediction, son. Now, sit down and prepare yourself for a breakfast feast."

"You bet, Dad," Marcus answered, plopping down at the table made of one round cut of a gigantic tree trunk. The wood with all its yearly rings had been sanded and polished to a gleaming finish and then coated with **polyurethane**.

Rusty scrambled eggs, which sizzled in the cast iron frying pan. He popped four chunks of wheat bread into the toaster, and set a bowl of fresh apples and bananas on the table. Marcus grabbed a banana and ate it as he considered the quiet **efficiency** of his father. The meal wasn't fancy, but his father moved solidly one step to the next, delivering steaming eggs and hot toast to the table without delay.

"Delicious, Dad," Marcus commented as he finished his eggs and three pieces of toast. He gulped a huge bite of juicy apple. "This is great! Tastes like apples in the orchard. Must be 'cause we're out here in the woods."

"Must be," Rusty repeated. "Now, finish that one and get some lunch packed—about six water bottles, those wheat crackers, the cheese, a knife, some of that fruit if you like—while I make your favorite: tuna and tomato sandwiches."

"Hey, I'm hungry already," Marcus teased lightly.

When the lunch was packed, Rusty and Marcus put on jackets, baseball caps, and beach sandals and headed out to the canoe with the lunch, binoculars, safety vests, **flotation** cushions, and oars. The canoe was tied to a post near a **dilapidated** dock.

Rusty pulled the canoe to the water's edge, loaded it, told Marcus to get in, and then eased the canoe farther into the water, jumping in at the last possible moment as lightly as a songbird. Keeping low, he settled in the stern and began to paddle. Marcus, in the bow, paddled on the other side to guide the canoe straight out onto the lake.

The morning passed as beautifully as it had looked from the cabin window. Only a soft summer breeze brushed the trees along the shore, so that branches barely swayed. The father and son paddled for intervals, stopping in between to let the canoe float aimlessly along. After noon, Rusty suggested they head for Knoll Island for lunch. Marcus heartily agreed.

Completing a plot-line prediction diagram

Some of this plot-line prediction diagram for the first part of the short story has been filled in. Add the events that follow these and make a prediction about what will happen next in the story.

> Rusty wakes and awakens Marcus.

> They plan on an all-day canoe trip.

> Rusty checks the forecast.

> Rusty fixes breakfast, and they eat.

>

>

>

PREDICTION

>

Read the second part of the short story "Ripples on Lake Juniper."

Rusty and Marcus glided to the island, secured the canoe to a tree, and ate lunch. Then they lay back on the dry pine-needled ground and stared at the **azure** sky. Now and then, a chickadee flirted by or a nuthatch dashed from one tree to another.

"Let's get back on the lake," Marcus suggested lazily. He stretched, then helped his dad pack up their trash to carry back. Rusty made sure the island looked just as it did—actually better than it did—when they arrived. He collected a soda can someone had uncaringly thrown behind a bush and tucked it into the trash.

The sun sat high and bright, and the surface of the lake was mirrorlike. The two canoed for about an hour before Rusty spotted a large bird standing in the water near the far shore. "I think I see a heron. Check it out, Marcus." They stopped rowing, and the boat slipped along toward the still faraway bird. Marcus picked up the binoculars and focused on the spot his father had pointed to.

"Got it! It's a great blue," Marcus announced.

"Let's see if we can sneak in for a closer look," Rusty suggested. "I'll paddle." He dipped the oar into the water and paddled silently. The only sound was the drip, drip, drip of the water as he lifted the oar for the next stroke.

"Dad, how can you paddle so quietly?" Marcus asked.

"Practice, son. Now let's be quiet ourselves."

Marcus kept the binoculars focused as they drifted closer to the bird. It was standing on one leg with the other tucked up. Its gray-blue **plumage** shone in the sun. The canoers drew close enough to see the strong beak and then the red eyes. Rusty stopped rowing and held the oar steady and still. The canoe slipped forward with the remaining **momentum**.

"We're within fifty feet," Marcus whispered. "It's a giant!" His father glared at him to remind him to be silent. Forty-five feet. Forty feet. The canoe slid closer but slower. Thirty-five feet. Then suddenly, the great wings of the heron stretched outward and the legs pushed and the bird lifted into the air with tremendously long and graceful wing beats, its long neck reaching forward. It flew directly over the canoe, as if to say, I knew you were there all along. The bird continued about two hundred feet in the other direction and then landed as gracefully as a glider.

For part of the afternoon, the canoers respectfully played tag with the heron, following its flights quietly as it leaped from one place to the next. The game ended when the heron flew far off to the west. Then Rusty and Marcus paddled to a group of small islands and explored the inlets and peninsulas, startling ducks that quacked into flight like dry leaves blown by a gusty wind.

Late in the afternoon, Rusty looped around to direct the canoe back toward the cabin. Ahead, in the widest section of Lake Juniper, the water pulsed in silvery ripples. Rusty drifted along the shoreline and then cut out toward the middle to cross the lake. Marcus picked up his oar and began paddling **absent-mindedly**. But when they entered the ripples, a wind blasted from ahead and they found themselves blown backward. Rusty paddled hard, and ordered Marcus to do the same. Still, progress was slow and **tedious**. The sun rushed toward the horizon, threatening the team with darkness.

"Will we get back before dark?" Marcus **queried** nervously.

"Well, if we let the wind blow us toward the opposite shore, we can follow the shoreline, but then it will certainly be very dark before we find the cabin—if we can find it," Rusty answered seriously. Marcus frowned. "Or, we can paddle and wait until our passage becomes clear."

"Clear. How will it become clear?" Marcus demanded. His dad smiled and glanced toward the disappearing sun.

Using a plot-line prediction diagram

Fill in the plot-line prediction diagram with important events from the second part of the story. Then make a prediction about what will happen.

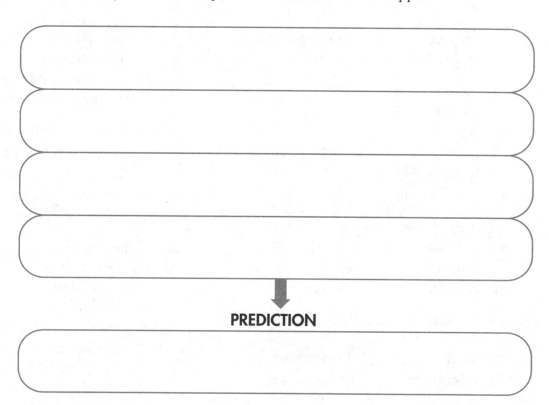

PREDICTION

Check Your Understanding

Think about what you've read. Then answer these questions.

1. What will probably happen in the next part of the story?
   - (A) Rusty and Marcus will spend an unpleasant night on the lake without food, water, or warm clothing.
   - (B) Rusty will allow the canoe to be blown to the far shore and then paddle back to the cabin in the dark along the shoreline.
   - (C) Marcus will panic and tip over the canoe as evening gets darker and darker.
   - (D) Rusty will wait until the wind dies after sunset and paddle through the middle of the lake back to the cabin.

2. What do you think would have happened if they had paddled loudly to approach the heron?
   - (A) They would have gotten much closer because they would have been moving faster.
   - (B) The heron would have flown off much sooner, startled by the noise.
   - (C) Several herons would have flown in to see what all the noise was about.
   - (D) They would have had to turn to avoid hitting the heron.

3. You should not trust the safety of a dock that
   - (A) is tedious.
   - (B) has any wood coated with polyurethane.
   - (C) looks dilapidated.
   - (D) displays plumage.

4. A person who works quickly but absent-mindedly is likely to lack
   - (A) flotation.
   - (B) efficiency.
   - (C) momentum.
   - (D) carnelian.

5. Which word completes the analogy?
   mammal:fur::bird:_____
   - (A) azure
   - (B) momentum
   - (C) flotation
   - (D) plumage

6. What is the main idea of the story?
   - (A) Observing nature can help you to overcome a possible crisis.
   - (B) Canoeing can be very risky and difficult.
   - (C) The weather can always change, so don't go out canoeing all day.
   - (D) Working together can sometimes prevent a nasty accident.

7. What causes the unusual silvery ripples in the middle of the lake?
   - (A) a fast-moving current
   - (B) a storm
   - (C) a strong wind
   - (D) a huge fish

8. Which sentence is the best summary of the story?
   - (A) A temperamental father and son must learn to cooperate to save their lives.
   - (B) A father and son enjoy a fine day canoeing and face a solvable challenge getting back to their cabin.
   - (C) A father teaches his son that chasing birds on a lake can cause one to travel too far from their cabin.
   - (D) A son reminds his father that safety on the water is very important.

9. The purpose of this story is to
   - (A) persuade you to try canoeing.
   - (B) inform you about water birds.
   - (C) describe a beautiful lake.
   - (D) entertain you and teach you a lesson.

10. In the first paragraph on page 60, the author says that "a chickadee flirted by." What is meant by *flirted*?
    - (A) The bird flitted about lightly and playfully.
    - (B) The bird blinked its eyes as it passed.
    - (C) The bird raced by almost faster than the eye could follow.
    - (D) The bird landed near Rusty and Marcus and sang loudly.

11. In the next to last paragraph on page 60, "landed as gracefully as a glider" compares

Ⓐ the drifting canoe to a landing airplane.

Ⓑ the landing of the heron to that of an engineless aircraft.

Ⓒ the heron gliding over the water to the gliding canoe.

Ⓓ the bird's landing to an ice skater's glide after jumping.

12. What happened next after the heron flew off for the first time?

Ⓐ Rusty and Marcus canoed into the inlets and around the peninsulas.

Ⓑ Rusty and Marcus stopped for lunch at Knoll Island.

Ⓒ Rusty and Marcus paddled into the ripply water.

Ⓓ Rusty and Marcus kept quietly creeping up on the heron until it flew far off to the west.

Extend Your Learning

- *Complete a Story*

    Work with a group to plan a series of events up to but not including the last event in the story "Ripples on Lake Juniper." List your plot events on a plot-line prediction diagram. Then have each group member write in a prediction for the final event of the story. Discuss the predictions and decide which one you want to use for your story ending. As a group, write an ending to the story and share it with another group.

- *Use a Plot-line Prediction Diagram*

    Work with any story or novel you are reading at the time. Create a plot-line diagram for the whole narrative or the chapter you are reading. Then add a prediction for the next part of the narrative. As you read, check the accuracy of your prediction. If you were wrong, go back to see if you missed some clues the author had provided or if you mistook the purpose of certain events or actions. Try to understand why your prediction was wrong.

- *Write Your Own Short Story*

    Think of a series of events with lots of action around which to build a story. Plan on using two or more characters, one or more settings, and at least ten plot events. (You can list your events in a plot-line prediction diagram.) Think of an idea about life that you want to suggest by the actions, events, and outcomes of your story. That will be your theme. Write your story, describing and developing your characters, detailing your setting, and laying out your series of events to teach your lesson about life. Add a picture to accompany your story and post your story on the board or in a collection of classmates' stories for all to read.

Finding Word Meaning in Context

Learn About Finding Word Meaning in Context

Thinking about the strategy

When you read, you often encounter a word that you do not know. What do you usually do? Most times, you probably read on to see if you can figure out the meaning of the word. When you do this, you use **context clues**, the words around an unknown word, to find word meaning.

Suppose you read this sentence in a history book: "The colonial militia rallied to the cause, defeating the British troops after a long battle." You may not be certain, but you can guess that *colonial* has to do with the colonies established on the North American continent from the 1600s to the 1700s. *Militia* must be soldiers since they fight British troops. *Rallied* suggests working together and regathering strength; you can tell this because the militia defeats the British after a long battle. Finally, you can guess that since it's a colonial/British conflict, the *cause* is independence from Great Britain.

You can use context clues for all kinds of reading and listening. Look for synonyms or antonyms the author may use to help you understand the unknown word. Look for a definition in the reading selection or an explanation of the word. Look at what the whole selection is about. Finally think about what you already know.

Studying a model

Read the passage by Benjamin Franklin and the notes beside it.

An Adaptation from *The Autobiography*

Anecdotes *may be an unfamiliar word, but from the context, they must be interesting stories.*

"Remains of my relations" does not use the word remains *to mean "bodies." You would not get information from bodies but from relatives remaining alive.*

Particulars must be facts or details from the anecdotes because they relate to ancestors and are in the notes.

Smith's is not a name here, but a business, or trade.

I have ever had a pleasure in obtaining any little anecdotes of my ancestors. You may remember the inquiries I made among the remains of my relations when you were with me in England, and the journey I undertook for that purpose. Now imagining it may be equally agreeable to you to know the circumstances of my life, many of which you are yet unacquainted with, and expecting a week's uninterrupted leisure in my present country retirement, I sit down to write them for you.

The notes of one of my uncles (who had the same curiosity in collecting family anecdotes) once put into my hands furnished me with several particulars relating to our ancestors. From these notes I learned that the family had lived in the same village, Ecton, in Northamptonshire, for three hundred years, and how much longer he knew not on a freehold of about thirty acres, aided by the smith's business, which had continued in the family till his time.

Learn About a Graphic Organizer

*Understanding
a context clue chart*

A **context clue chart** helps you study the words that are new to you in a passage. It helps you determine the meaning of any words that are used in an unfamiliar way. Your effort enables you to understand the passage as a whole.

Here is a context clue chart for the first paragraph of the passage on page 64.

List all the words that you are not sure of because they are new to you or have a different meaning than usual.

Put all the information you have about the word: what the words around it suggest, related phrases from the passage, similar words you already know.

Guess at the meaning of the word and then see how that meaning applies to the reading. If you are still uncertain about the exact meaning, use a dictionary to check your guess.

Word	Context Clues/What I Know	Meaning
anecdotes	obtains them from relatives now is telling his own story	interesting stories
inquiries	made of relatives *inquire* means "to ask"	questions
remains	of relations he speaks to	ones left alive
retirement	usually means stopping work week's leisure	rest, vacation

A context clue chart helps you understand the meaning of new words that in turn help you understand the passage.

What kind of retirement is the author talking about?
A week's vacation in the country.

As you read, ask yourself

- What words around the unknown word help suggest its meaning?
- What similar words do I already know that help me understand the word in this context?
- Does the author give a synonym or an antonym, a definition, or an explanation?
- Does the purpose of the selection help make the meaning clear?

Learn About a Form of Writing

Focusing on an autobiography

An **autobiography** is the story, or narrative, of a person's life told by that person. (A biography is the story of a person's life told by another person.) Because it is a story, an autobiography has a beginning, a middle, and an ending. The beginning may be birth and/or early childhood experiences; the middle may be about the days of youth; and the ending may bring the reader up to the present in the person's life. (In a biography, the ending may be the person's death.)

An autobiography has these characteristics.

- An autobiography is a narrative.
- The story is nonfiction about someone who really lived.
- The author's life is the subject of the story.
- The story is set when and where the person lived.
- The story is generally told in the first person, using the pronouns *I* and *me*.
- The author often reveals thoughts and feelings as well as events and experiences.

Organizing ideas in a context clue chart

You can use a context clue chart for any form of writing, including an autobiography.

Here is a context clue chart for the second paragraph of the autobiographical passage on page 64.

Word	Context Clues/What I Know	Meaning
particulars	notes provided uncle collected family stories	facts or details about
freehold	about thirty acres free suggests "not slave or rented"	personal land
smith's	business part of *blacksmith* or *goldsmith*	metalworker

A context clue chart for the passage helps you understand the meaning of the paragraph as you interpret the meaning of the new and unusual words.

Prepare for the Reading Selection

Gaining knowledge

Almost everyone makes use of autobiographical writing. If you keep a journal or a diary, you record events and happenings, as well as thoughts and feelings about your life. If you write letters or e-mails to friends and family, they probably contain autobiographical information. But these forms—diaries, journals, letters—are not complete nor usually meant for the public to read. People who want to tell their own story often write organized autobiographies. Some write them for themselves or their family; others write for the general reader.

Benjamin Franklin was an American who lived from 1706–1790. At 16, when his brother was jailed for offending authorities with articles in his *New England Courant*, 16-year-old Benjamin successfully took over the paper. That was just the start of his many careers in printing, writing (including *Poor Richard's Almanack*), science, politics, and inventing. During his lifetime, many changes occurred in America. Franklin himself promoted changes: the first circulating library, the first colonial hospital, the first scholarly society (the American Philosophical Society), to name a few. He is also well-known for his work with electricity and his participation in the Constitutional Convention. When he was 65, Franklin began *The Autobiography*, his account of his first 24 years, written for his son. Franklin was later persuaded to continue writing, but he only wrote of his experiences through 1759. The account ended before the time of his intense involvement in public service and international diplomacy. On the following pages, you will read excerpts from his autobiography.

Learn Vocabulary

Understanding vocabulary

The boxed words below are **boldfaced** in the selection. Learn the meaning of each word. Then write the word beside its clue.

bred
inclination
hankering
approbation
contrived
anonymous
exquisite
assert
mortification

1. _____ a leaning toward something, the noun form of *to incline* "to lean, to show an interest in"

2. _____ unknown in name

3. _____ to state or express positively

4. _____ praise, from Latin *approbare*, "to approve"

5. _____ longing, desiring

6. _____ shame, humiliation, intense distress, from Latin *mortifcare*, "to cause to die"

7. _____ planned cleverly; also plotted evilly

8. _____ developed, trained by the family

9. _____ intense; also beautifully made or designed

Read the first part of the autobiography excerpt adapted from *The Autobiography* by Benjamin Franklin.

An Adaptation from *The Autobiography*

At ten years old I was taken home from school to assist my father in business, which was that of a tallow-chandler and soapboiler; a business he was not **bred** to, but had assumed on his arrival in New England, on finding his dying trade would not maintain his family, being in little request. Accordingly, I was employed in cutting wicks for the candles, filling the dipping molds and the molds for cast candles, attending the shop, and going on errands.

From a child I was fond of reading, and all the little money that came into my hands was ever laid out on books. Pleased with the *Pilgrim's Progress,* my first collection was of John Bunyan's works in separate little volumes. I afterwards sold them to enable me to buy R. Burton's *Historical Collections*; they were small books, and cheap, forty or fifty in all.

The bookish **inclination** at length determined my father to make me a printer, though he had already one son (James) of the profession. In 1717 my brother James returned from England with a press and letters to set up his business in Boston. I liked the business much better than that of my father, but I still had a **hankering** for the sea. To prevent the feared effect of such an inclination, my father was impatient to have me bound to my brother. I held out some time, but at last was persuaded, and signed the indentures when I was yet but twelve years old.

After some time an ingenious tradesman, Mr. Matthew Adams, who had a pretty collection of books, and who frequented our printing-house, took notice of me, invited me to his library, and very kindly lent me such books as I chose to read. I now took a fancy to poetry, and wrote some little pieces; my brother encouraged me, and put me on composing two occasional ballads. One was called *The Lighthouse Tragedy* and the other was a sailor's song. These were printed but my father discouraged me, telling me verse-makers were generally beggars.

My brother had some ingenious men among his friends, who amused themselves by writing little pieces for his paper. Hearing their conversations, and their accounts of the **approbation** their papers were received with, I was excited to try my hand among them; but, being still a boy, and suspecting that my brother would object to printing anything of mine in his paper if he knew it to be mine, I **contrived** to disguise my hand and, writing an **anonymous** paper, I put it in at night under the door of the printing-house. It was found in the morning and communicated to his writing friends when they called in as usual. They read it, commented on it in my hearing, and I had the **exquisite** pleasure of finding it met with their approbation. My brother printed it and several more over time without knowing they were mine.

At length, differences began arising between my brother and me. I took upon me to **assert** my freedom since he had long since disposed of my first indentures. When he found I would leave him, he took care to prevent my getting employment in any printing-house of the town, by going around and speaking to every master, who accordingly refused to give me work.

Completing a context clue chart

Some of this context clue chart for the first part of the autobiography excerpt has been filled in. Add more information for the words listed.

Word	Context Clues/What I Know	Meaning
tallow-chandler	cutting wicks for candles this is a business	candle maker
soapboiler	has <u>soap</u> and <u>boil</u> in it	
press	to set up a business he's a printer	
letters		
bound	has to do with brother's shop would keep Franklin home	
indentures		
occasional ballads		
hand		

Read the second part of the autobiography excerpt adapted from *The Autobiography* by Benjamin Franklin.

I then thought of going to New York, as the nearest place where there was a printer. So I sold some of my books to raise a little money, got on a private boat arranged by a friend, and as we had a fair wind, in three days I found myself in New York, nearly three hundred miles from home, a boy of but seventeen, without the least recommendation to, or knowledge of, any person in the place, and with very little money in my pocket.

But, having a trade, and supposing myself a pretty good workman, I offered my service to the printer of the place, old Mr. William Bradford. He had no work, but said his son in Philadelphia had need of someone. Philadelphia was one hundred miles further. I set out, however, in a boat for Perth Amboy, leaving my chest and things to follow me round by sea. In the morning I started on foot fifty miles to Burlington, where I was told I should find boats that would carry me the rest of the way to Philadelphia.

It rained very hard all the day: I was thoroughly soaked, and by noon a good deal tired; so I stopped at a poor inn, where I stayed all night, beginning now to wish I had never left home. However, I proceeded the next day, and got in the evening to an inn, within eight or ten miles of Burlington. At this inn I stayed the night, and the next morning reached Burlington, but had the **mortification** to find that the regular boats were gone a little before my coming, and no other expected to go till Tuesday, this being Saturday. Yet after eating a dinner, I encountered a rowboat on the river heading for Philadelphia, and I asked to go aboard.

I have been the more particular in this description of my journey, and shall be so of my first entry into Philadelphia, that you may in your mind compare such unlikely beginnings with the figure I have since made there. I arrived in my working dress, my best clothes being to come round by sea. I was dirty from my journey. My pockets were stuffed out with shirts and stockings. I knew not a soul nor where to look for lodging. I was fatigued with traveling, rowing, and want of rest. I was very hungry; and my whole cash consisted of a Dutch dollar and about a shilling in copper. The latter I gave the people of the boat for my passage; I insisted on their taking it, a man being sometimes more generous when he has but little money than when he has plenty, perhaps through fear of being thought to have little.

Then I walked up the street, gazing about, till near the market house I met a boy with bread. I had made many a meal on bread, and, inquiring where he got it, I went immediately to the bakers he directed me to, in Second Street, and asked for biscuit, intending such as we had in Boston. But they, it seems, were not made in Philadelphia. Then I asked for a three-penny loaf, and was told they had none such. So, not considering or knowing the difference of money, and the greater cheapness nor the names of his bread, I bade him give me three-penny worth of any sort. He gave me three great puffy rolls.

I was surprised at the quantity, but took it, and having no room in my pockets, walked off with a roll under each arm, and eating the other. Thus I went up Market Street as far as Fourth Street, passing the door of Mr. Read, my future wife's father; then she, standing at the door, saw me, and thought I made, as I certainly did, a most awkward, ridiculous appearance. Then I turned and went down Chestnut Street and part of Walnut Street, eating my roll all the way, and coming round, found myself again at Market Street wharf, near the rowboat. Being filled with one of my rolls, I gave the other two to a woman and child who had come down the river in the boat with me.

Using a context clue chart

Fill in your own context clue chart for the second part of the autobiography excerpt. Consider using these words as well as any others that are new or unfamiliar to you: *trade, chest, round by sea, particular, figure, working dress, shilling, three-penny loaf.* If you need more space, use another piece of paper.

Word	Context Clues/What I Know	Meaning

Check Your Understanding

Think about what you've read. Then answer these questions.

1. In the last paragraph on page 68, Franklin uses the word *ingenious* to describe men his brother knows. Use the context to help select the best meaning for *ingenious*.
   - Ⓐ "clever and inventive"
   - Ⓑ "simple and innocent"
   - Ⓒ "bothersome and annoying"
   - Ⓓ "friendly and helpful"

2. In the paragraph on page 69, Franklin says "differences began arising between my brother and me." By differences, he means
   - Ⓐ changes in size and shape.
   - Ⓑ quarrels and disagreements.
   - Ⓒ mathematical calculations.
   - Ⓓ variations in ability.

3. A person would most likely have a hankering for
   - Ⓐ an accident.
   - Ⓑ poison.
   - Ⓒ fruit.
   - Ⓓ a cold.

4. Which word completes the analogy?
   mortification:shame::_____ :praise
   - Ⓐ approbation
   - Ⓒ exquisite
   - Ⓑ contrived
   - Ⓓ inclination

5. If a book publishes a poem but the author is not known, the poem may be identified as
   - Ⓐ contrived.
   - Ⓑ bred.
   - Ⓒ approbation.
   - Ⓓ anonymous.

6. What caused Franklin's father to make Franklin a printer?
   - Ⓐ Franklin did not like his father's business.
   - Ⓑ Franklin's brother was a printer.
   - Ⓒ Franklin liked books.
   - Ⓓ Franklin's father had found out how much money printers made.

7. What happened after Franklin reached Burlington?
   - Ⓐ He asked Mr. William Bradford for printing work.
   - Ⓑ He stayed at an inn overnight.
   - Ⓒ He set out in a boat for Perth Amboy, leaving his chest to follow round by sea.
   - Ⓓ He discovered that the regular boats to Philadelphia had already left.

8. The main idea Franklin wants to show in his autobiography is stated in the fourth paragraph on page 70. Which sentence is the best statement of the main idea?
   - Ⓐ From rough beginnings and difficulties, you can make something of yourself.
   - Ⓑ When you have disagreements with your family, these disagreements can ruin your life.
   - Ⓒ People always expect you to be the way you were when they first saw you.
   - Ⓓ You cannot succeed in life by running away from your home and family.

9. What can you conclude about food prices in Philadelphia compared to Boston?
   - Ⓐ Food was much cheaper in Philadelphia.
   - Ⓑ Food was much more expensive in Philadelphia.
   - Ⓒ The prices were almost exactly the same.
   - Ⓓ There is no evidence one way or the other in the selection.

10. What reason does Franklin give for insisting that the man take money for his passage to Philadelphia?
    - Ⓐ Franklin didn't want to look ungrateful for the ride.
    - Ⓑ The man was poor.
    - Ⓒ Franklin was dressed well so he didn't want to appear stingy.
    - Ⓓ Franklin didn't want people to think he had little money.

11. What do you predict Franklin will try to do next?

Ⓐ Contact his family in Boston and let them know where he is.

Ⓑ Look for Mr. Bradford's son and try to get a job at his print shop.

Ⓒ Go back to the bakery and buy several more three-penny loaves.

Ⓓ Go to Mr. Read's home and introduce himself as Benjamin Franklin.

12. Which sentence part from the autobiography excerpt expresses an opinion?

Ⓐ Thus I went up Market Street as far as Fourth Street,

Ⓑ passing the door of Mr. Read, my future wife's father;

Ⓒ then she, standing at the door, saw me,

Ⓓ and thought I made, as I certainly did, a most awkward, ridiculous appearance.

Extend Your Learning

- *Write Your Autobiography*

  Think of a time when you did something that was a bit frightening or difficult. Write an autobiographical sketch to describe the incident, telling what you did and how you felt. Include in your sketch what you would hope others could learn from your experience. Share your sketch with a classmate or friend.

- *Use a Context Clue Chart*

  Use a science or social studies textbook or other reading you have to complete for school. Work with a group of students who have the same assigned work. Together, create a context clue chart in which you list new words from the reading, write the clues and what you know, and guess at the meanings. Use the dictionary or glossary in the textbook to check your accuracy.

- *Present Benjamin Franklin*

  Work in groups to find out more about some of Benjamin Franklin's many accomplishments. Create short skits or monologues about Franklin, such as Franklin at the Constitutional Convention or Franklin experimenting with electricity. Select actors and present your skits. Use costumes and props if you want.

Drawing Conclusions and Making Inferences

Learn About Drawing Conclusions and Making Inferences

Thinking about the strategy

Authors don't tell you every detail about the characters, setting, and events in a story. Authors expect that you will be able to **draw conclusions** and **make inferences** about things that are not stated outright. A conclusion or inference is what you determine to be probably true based on what you do know.

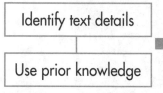

Identify text details
Use prior knowledge

→ Draw a conclusion
or
Make an inference

To draw a conclusion or make an inference, combine details from the text with prior knowledge. Prior knowledge includes information that you know from your life experiences; what you know about the world in general; and what you may have learned from facts and details presented earlier in the text.

Studying a model

Read this passage from a fiction story and the notes beside it.

Questions about details:

Why do Kristy and her mom cover the windows with plywood?

Why is the surf roaring? Why is the wind getting stronger?

Where do Kristy and her mom live?

What probably happened to their neighbors' homes? What is Mom's worst fear?

What happened to Dad?

"We've covered all the windows with plywood," Kristy hollered, trying to be heard above the roaring surf. "What should we do now?"

"I'm not sure," her mom shouted back. "Pray that the seawall holds, I guess."

"What if it doesn't?" Kristy asked. The wind, which was already getting stronger, whipped off her hood. Her long black hair flew about her head wildly.

"We may have no choice but to evacuate," Kristy's mom responded. She gazed down the slippery sandy slope that led to the sea and recalled with horror what had happened to three of their neighbors' homes last hurricane season. She didn't voice her worst fears to Kristy.

"I wish Dad were here," Kristy said sadly. She bit her lip and tried not to cry. "He would know what to do."

"He always did," her mom responded with a wistful smile.

Learn About a Graphic Organizer

Understanding a conclusions/inferences diagram

For a conclusion or inference to be valid it must be based on details in the text. A **conclusions/inferences diagram** can help you identify details that the author provides so that you can arrive at reasonable, valid conclusions and inferences about the characters, setting, and important events in a story.

Here is a conclusions/inferences diagram for the passage on page 74.

STORY DETAILS	CONCLUSIONS/INFERENCES
Kristy says, "We've covered all the windows with plywood." Mom says, "Pray that the seawall holds." The wind is getting stronger. Mom recalls last hurricane season.	Kristy and her mom are preparing for a hurricane.
Kristy hollers above the roaring surf. Mom gazes down the slippery slope to the sea.	Kristy and her mom live on a seacoast.
Mom recalls in horror what happened to her neighbors' homes. She doesn't voice her worst fears.	Mom is worried that their home could slip into the sea.
Kristy is sad as she wishes her dad were there. Mom has a wistful smile.	Dad has probably died.

Keep in mind that conclusions or inferences that are not supported with details in the text are invalid. If your conclusions and inferences are invalid, you are apt to become confused as you read. For example, based on the details that the author provides in the passage, a valid conclusion is that Kristy's dad has probably died. An invalid conclusion would be that Kristy's dad died in an accident at sea during a hurricane. None of the details in the text suggests that that is true.

As you read, ask yourself

- What details does the author tell me?
- What information does the author leave out?
- What prior knowledge do I have?
- What can I figure out to be probably true?

Learn About a Form of Writing

Focusing on a journal/diary writing

Journal/diary writing is a form of reflective writing in which writers record their own thoughts, feelings, and reactions to the people, places, and events that they encounter. Journals and diaries are usually intended to be personal and private. Some are published, although professional writers are more likely to use their journal writing as a way to explore topics and ideas for other forms of writing.

Journal or diary writing has the following characteristics.

- The writing is personal and informal.
- The entries are usually dated, cover somewhat regular time intervals, and tell about people, places, and events encountered during that time period.
- The information is written from the first-person point of view, using the personal pronoun *I*.
- Entries highlight personal observations and feelings but may also include facts and details about people, places, and events.

Organizing ideas in a conclusions/inferences diagram

Journal or diary writers are basically talking to themselves as they reflect on people, places, and events that have made an impression on them. As a result, they do not include every single detail related to those people, places, and events, but just those details that are especially significant and memorable. That means readers must ask themselves questions about the details that the writer does include—they must draw conclusions and make inferences.

A conclusions/inferences diagram like this one can help you check your own understanding of the details you identify in a journal or diary entry.

STORY DETAILS	CONCLUSIONS/INFERENCES
descriptive details about people, places, and events	unstated relationships between details
what people say and do	understanding based on prior knowledge
personal reactions to people, places, and events	reasonable beliefs
thoughts about people, places, and events	

Prepare for the Reading Selection

Have you ever heard someone describe an event that you witnessed and then wondered if the other person was actually there because his or her description of the event is so different from yours? People's reactions reflect their personal preferences, attitudes, and life history. As a result, two people can have totally opposite recollections of the same event.

The pages that follow contain fictional journal entries by two writers. These entries discuss similar people, places, and events. The description of these people, places, and events reflects the perspective, or viewpoint, of the individual writer. As you read, notice how the personality of each writer is revealed through the details that the writer chooses.

Learn Vocabulary

The boxed words below are **boldfaced** in the selection. Learn the meaning of each word. Then write the word that is a synonym of the pair of words.

| horrendous |
| infamous |
| ironic |
| emits |
| camouflage |
| appease |
| defensive |
| lament |
| aroma |

1. _____ gives out, produces

2. _____ complain, moan about

3. _____ soothe, calm

4. _____ well-known, familiar

5. _____ self-protective, suspicious

6. _____ terrible, awful

7. _____ smell, scent

8. _____ absurd, unreasonable

9. _____ hide, disguise

Read the first journal entry "Marc's Journal."

Marc's Journal

April 14

I'm supposed to keep a journal for my writing class. This feels wimpy to me, but I have been told that I need to have a B average to stay on the baseball team, so here goes.

Today got off to a **horrendous** start. First, I missed the bus—by two measly seconds. Mr. Adams could have opened the door, but I think he was trying to teach me a lesson. I'm sure he's had it in for me since I told his daughter Annie that I already had a date to the spring formal, which was the truth at the time. Anyway, I had to go back in the house and ask my dad to drive me to school. It's on his way to work, so it's not as if I was taking him out of his way. For the entire drive (which seemed more like two hours than fifteen minutes), I had to listen to one of his **infamous** lectures about responsibility. Today's was one of my personal favorites. It's the one about how if I would only follow his example, I wouldn't constantly have to ask him or Mom for rides to school, baseball practice, and guitar lessons. Right, if only I was as uptight and rigid as Dad, then my life would be perfect. I can't wait until I'm old enough to drive. Meanwhile, Dad says that unless I get my act together that'll never happen.

What's really **ironic** and so very typical is that Julie was in the car, too. Did Dad lecture his little darling? No, of course not. It didn't seem to dawn on him that—duh?—she had missed the bus, too. But then I'm the one who always messes up so I guess I deserved it. When we got to school, Julie gave Dad a big hug and kiss, thanked him "oodles," and then jumped out of the car. He smiled and told her to have a wonderful day. He told me to stand up straight and to stay out of trouble.

Julie was waiting for me on the school steps. She was wearing her "sweet little sister" smile, but I didn't feel like a lecture from her, too. So I brushed past her. As usual she wouldn't let it go. "Why don't you try lightening up?" she said.

"Why don't you spend a little less time looking at yourself in the bathroom mirror," I snapped back. "I didn't even have time to take a shower!"

She was about to give me some lame excuse when I spotted Nick and ran to catch up with him in the hall. "You weren't on the bus," he said. Nick has an amazing grasp of the obvious. "Pete said Mr. Adams saw you in his rear view mirror and snickered when he saw you running to catch the bus."

I shook my head and told Nick I'd meet him in the cafeteria at lunch. Then I headed into the lab. I have science first thing on Monday mornings, and my dear sister is in my honors science class even though she is a year behind me and two years younger. We usually sit together, but today I wanted no part of her, so I took the empty seat beside Wilbur Ross. There's always an empty seat beside Wilbur, who **emits** a strange sweet odor that no one has ever been able to identify. Chris Shields asked him about it once. Wilbur said it was the fabric softener that his mother uses in the laundry. Wilbur would be your typical science nerd except for two things. First, he is the best pitcher on the school baseball team. Second, he can sing. I mean SING. He's the lead singer for the amazing Blue Rock Chickens, one of our school's best rock bands.

The rest of the day dragged. All day I had this feeling that I'd done something wrong when all I'd done was miss the bus. If I was actually in control of my own life, I'd probably never miss the bus again. I have a plan though that should make Dad proud. Tomorrow, I'm getting into the bathroom before Julie. I'll let you know how it goes.

Completing a conclusions/ inferences diagram

Draw conclusions and make inferences based on the story details so far. Fill in the missing parts of the conclusions/inferences diagram.

STORY DETAILS	CONCLUSIONS/INFERENCES
	Marc is not thrilled about having to keep a journal.
Marc listens to one of Dad's infamous lectures about responsibility. Today's was a personal favorite.	
	Marc plays on a baseball team, and he is learning to play the guitar.
Did Dad lecture his little darling?	
	Marc admires Wilbur Ross.
Marc says, "If I was actually in control of my own life, I'd probably never miss the bus again."	

Julie's Journal

April 14

Why do teenagers have to get zits? Why don't old married people who already have someone to go out with and don't have to care what they look like get zits? I do all the things I'm supposed to do to have clear skin. I exercise. I eat lots of vegetables and fruit. I scrub my face with that disgusting, smelly stuff that Mom got me from the doctor. I keep my hands and my hair off my face. None of it matters. What's really unfair is that Marc has perfectly clear, beautiful skin. And he eats greasy burgers, chips, and fries—all the time! His hair (which is longer than mine) is always in his face. This morning I spent so much time in the bathroom trying to **camouflage** the huge eruptions on my forehead and chin that I made Marc late. He ended up missing the bus. We both did.

I asked Dad to take me to school. Dad can't understand why anyone has to be late for anything. So I started off by apologizing and promising to mow the lawn after school. That seemed to **appease** him. He was actually in a great mood until Marc came back in the house and asked for a ride, too. I'm pretty sure Dad wouldn't have made a big deal about it. After all, he had already agreed to take me, but Marc was so sullen and **defensive**. Dad doesn't believe teenagers have anything to be sullen about. "Wait until you have to go to work everyday for a boss who doesn't care if you're sick, or if you have a family emergency," he tells us all the time. "Then you can be sullen and defensive."

Marc's attitude set Dad off. The entire ride to school, he gave Marc the "be responsible, be more like me" speech. I was going to interrupt and tell Dad that it was my fault that Marc missed the bus, but Marc was giving me the most hateful looks. I think if Marc had thanked Dad for the ride when we got to school, Dad would have relented, but Marc just kept the attitude going. Dinner should be a treat tonight. I'd better warn Mom this time.

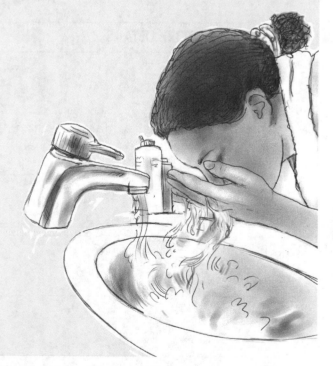

I waited for Marc on the school steps to tell him I was sorry, but he didn't want to hear it. Just wait until the next time he wants to **lament** about having to sit on the bench during a baseball game. I understand his frustration. I hate standing on the sidelines during a soccer game. I want to be out on the field for all 90 minutes.

I didn't realize how angry Marc was with me until I walked into the lab for science class. He was sitting next to Wilbur Ross. I like Wilbur. I'm one of the few people who doesn't notice his sweet **aroma**, and he's one of the few kids in honors science who thinks it's cool that I'm in the class even though I'm so much younger than everyone else. He's also secretly teaching me how to play guitar. Marc had said Wilbur didn't have the time. After school today, I went over to Wilbur's house for a lesson. He was practicing with his band, the Blue Rock Chickens. I guess I got my dates mixed up, but Wilbur told me to hang around anyway. Then guess what? He asked if I wanted to jam with the band. Wait until Marc hears that I got to play with the Blue Rock Chickens. Maybe I better not tell him for a few days. He's already mad at me.

I wonder if Wilbur has a date for the spring formal yet. . .

Using a conclusions/ inferences diagram

Fill in the conclusions/inferences diagram for the second journal entry, "Julie's Journal."

STORY DETAILS	CONCLUSIONS/INFERENCES

Check Your Understanding

Think about what you've read. Then answer these questions.

1. From what you have read, you can conclude that Marc and Julie
   Ⓐ argue all the time.
   Ⓑ would rather not be seen with each other.
   Ⓒ go to the same school.
   Ⓓ dislike Wilbur Ross.

2. Which of these is probably true based on what you know and details in the text?
   Ⓐ Marc's school requires students to maintain a B average to participate in sports and other after-school activities.
   Ⓑ Marc's parents will make him quit all extra-curricular activities unless he gets at least a B in writing.
   Ⓒ Marc hopes to play professional baseball someday.
   Ⓓ Marc does not get good grades in school.

3. Which word means the opposite of *horrendous*?
   Ⓐ mistaken
   Ⓑ miserable
   Ⓒ wonderful
   Ⓓ original

4. Something ironic is
   Ⓐ not what you would expect.
   Ⓑ sad and depressing.
   Ⓒ extremely amusing.
   Ⓓ challenging.

5. Which of these events happens first?
   Ⓐ Marc catches up with Nick in the school hall.
   Ⓑ Mr. Adams, the bus driver, snickers at Marc.
   Ⓒ Marc sits next to Wilbur Ross in science class.
   Ⓓ Julie tells Marc to lighten up.

6. According to Marc, why is Wilbur Ross not your typical science nerd?
   Ⓐ Julie is nice to Wilbur.
   Ⓑ Wilbur smells like laundry freshener.
   Ⓒ Wilbur is a great pitcher, and he can sing.
   Ⓓ Wilbur has an amazing grasp of the obvious.

7. From details in Marc's and Julie's journal entries, you can conclude that
   Ⓐ Dad probably plans his time carefully.
   Ⓑ Dad doesn't approve of his kids playing guitar.
   Ⓒ Dad hates his boss and is thinking of quitting.
   Ⓓ Dad has never been late for anything.

8. What does the word *eruptions* refer to in Julie's journal entry?
   Ⓐ ejection of lava from volcanoes
   Ⓑ sudden outbursts of yelling
   Ⓒ facial blemishes
   Ⓓ explosions of dynamite

9. Why does Julie think that Dad continues to lecture Marc on the ride to school?
   Ⓐ because Dad likes Julie better
   Ⓑ because of Marc's bad attitude
   Ⓒ because Dad thinks Marc should have promised to mow the lawn
   Ⓓ because Marc was giving Julie hateful looks

10. A defensive person usually wants to avoid
    Ⓐ sporting events.
    Ⓑ noise.
    Ⓒ sick people.
    Ⓓ criticism.

11. Which of these conclusions makes sense based on details in Julie's journal entry?

Ⓐ Julie is thinking about asking Wilbur to the spring formal.

Ⓑ Wilbur's band is playing at the spring formal.

Ⓒ Wilbur plans to ask Julie to the spring formal.

Ⓓ Wilbur has no intention of going to the spring formal.

12. From the details in Julie's journal entry, you can predict that Julie

Ⓐ will ask Wilbur if she can become a member of the Blue Rock Chickens.

Ⓑ will be a science teacher when she grows up.

Ⓒ will wait until Marc isn't mad to tell him about playing with the Blue Rock Chickens.

Ⓓ will not take so long in the bathroom ever again.

Extend Your Learning

- *Write a Journal Entry*

  What do you think will happen the next morning? What do you think will happen when Julie finally tells Marc that she played with the Blue Rock Chickens? Review the details in "Marc's Journal" and "Julie's Journal." Think about the conclusions and inferences you arrived at while reading. Then use those ideas and your imagination to write another journal entry for Marc and for Julie. When you have finished, share your journal entries with a partner. Discuss how your conclusions influenced what you wrote.

- *Read a Novel*

  Find a novel written as a journal or as a series of letters. As you read, use your own prior knowledge and the details the author gives to draw conclusions and make inferences about the characters, setting, and events in the novel. Jot down your ideas in a conclusions/inferences diagram.

- *Keep a Daily Journal*

  Write daily journal entries for a week. Include your thoughts, feelings, and reactions to the people, places, and events that you encounter each day. At the end of the week, go back and review your entries. Star ideas that you might like to explore later for fiction stories or nonfiction articles.

Distinguishing Between Fact and Opinion

Learn About Distinguishing Between Fact and Opinion

*Thinking about
the strategy*

A **fact** is a statement that can be proved true. You can check facts in a reliable source, such as an encyclopedia or a textbook. Facts can also be events that people experience or see with their own eyes. An **opinion** is a person's belief or judgment. People often use reasons and evidence, including facts, to support an opinion, but these do not make the opinion a fact.

Suppose you ask this question: "What was our math homework last night?" One classmate answers, "Pages 66–67, Problems 1–12." Another classmate responds, "The hardest problems we've ever had!" The first classmate stated a fact that you can prove by asking your math teacher. The second classmate offered an opinion. The opinion may turn out to be true for you or it may not, but no one can prove it one way or the other.

FACTS	Math	OPINION
Pages 66-67	**Homework**	hardest problems ever
Problems 1–12		

When you are reading or listening, you can recognize facts by thinking about which statements would have proof to back them up. Opinions often sound more personal. People may even introduce them with phrases such as *I think* or *many people agree*. Opinions often use superlatives such as *best, most, worst, wisest, most sensible*, and so on. They often include generalizing words such as *all, none, never, always*, or *often*.

Studying a model

Read the paragraph and the notes beside it.

Visit the United States

Facts about the size of the United States can be checked on a map.

Can you prove that the United States has the most and best land?

Think about the vastness of the United States. The mileage from the Atlantic to the Pacific coast is about 3,000. From the tip of Texas to Canada is about 1,600 miles. Hawaii lies in the Pacific and Alaska in the far North. In the United States, you will find the most and best land. No one needs more!

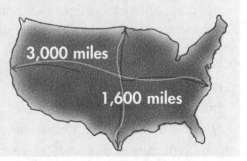

3,000 miles

1,600 miles

Learn About a Graphic Organizer

Understanding a fact/opinion chart

A **fact/opinion chart** can help you sort information into facts and opinions. Being able to identify facts and opinions will help you understand the author's purpose in a piece of writing.

Here is a fact/opinion chart for the paragraph on page 84. For a short selection, you can list almost all the facts and opinions. For a longer selection, you could organize your chart around main points.

These are statements that can be proved.

This is the issue being discussed.

These are what the author thinks and feels. The first makes a point about the land. The second suggests the main point of the paragraph.

FACTS		OPINIONS
Mileage from Atlantic to Pacific is about 3,000.	**Vastness of the United States**	In the U. S., you find the most and best land.
Texas to Canada is about 1,600 miles.		No one needs more!
Hawaii is in the Pacific and Alaska is in the far North.		

A fact/opinion chart displays the facts and opinions so that you can see exactly what kind of information you are reading. When you read *In the United States, you will find the most and best land*, you know that that is only one person's opinion.

As you read, ask yourself

- Is this information that can be proved?
- What source can I use to prove the statement?
- Is this one person's feeling about something?
- Do you find words that suggest opinions?

Learn About a Form of Writing

An **argumentative speech** supports one side of a debatable issue. The issue, often a personal feeling, is called the proposition. A proposition may state an opinion (often as if it were a fact) or suggest a particular action. The proposition, often a declarative sentence, is accompanied by facts, reasons, or additional opinions that support it. This evidence is an essential part of the argument, but often it is loaded with general statements that can't be proved and are meant to sway the listener to the speaker's point of view.

Look for the following characteristics of an argumentative speech.

- An argumentative speech is a spoken presentation.
- It discusses a point that has more than one possible side.
- It has a single purpose—to convince the listener of something.
- It generally states the purpose and provides evidence or reasoning to support it.

The paragraph on page 84 is the beginning of an argumentative speech. Read the final paragraph below. Look for the proposition of the speech in the paragraph. Then study the fact/opinion chart.

> That is why I say, "See this country first." You can find the most interesting landforms possible in the United States. The Rocky Mountains rise over 14,000 feet, while Death Valley rests at 282 feet below sea level. The Great Plains are the most fertile and beautiful plains in the world. Lake Superior is the second largest world lake. The islands of Hawaii are more relaxing than any others. Don't vacation in another country until you have seen the United States.

FACTS		OPINIONS
Rocky Mountains over 14,000 feet		most interesting landforms possible
Death Valley at 282 feet below sea level	**Seeing Types of Landforms**	Great Plains most fertile and beautiful in world
Lake Superior second largest lake		Hawaii more relaxing than other islands
		Don't vacation in another country until you have seen the United States.

The last opinion is the proposition of the argument.

A fact/opinion chart classifies the information so that you can easily see which part is fact and which is opinion. This helps you determine the merits of an argument. The chart also helps you find the main point of the argument.

Prepare for the Reading Selection

Gaining knowledge

Just about anything a person believes can be argued, but the arenas of life that lead to the most common arguments include religion and politics. Political arguments take the form of speeches, written essays, newspaper editorials and letters, debates, and even political cartoons.

One of the largest national "arguments" took place in Philadelphia in 1787, when delegates from all the new states except Rhode Island met to set up the government of the United States. At the Constitutional Convention, 55 men proposed and debated the duties and responsibilities of the branches of government. The decisions they made became the written Constitution of the United States. Since that time, 26 Amendments to the Constitution have been argued and passed, but much of the original plan stands. Today, people continue to debate whether certain parts of the Constitution, even certain Amendments, should be amended to reflect a new time period in the history of the country. The argumentative speech on the following pages is part of this debate.

Learn Vocabulary

Understanding vocabulary

The boxed words below are **boldfaced** in the selection. Learn the meaning of each word. Use a dictionary or social studies glossary to find the definition of each word or term. Then write a definition in your own words.

amendments
democratic
petition
Framers
electors
Electoral College
legislature
popular election
majority

1. amendments _____

2. democratic _____

3. petition _____

4. Framers _____

5. electors _____

6. Electoral College _____

7. legislature _____

8. popular election _____

9. majority _____

Read the first part of the argumentative speech "Let's Get Down to Democracy."

Let's Get Down to Democracy

Fellow Citizens, Educated Voters, Young People Who Want to Learn More About Their Country,

I am here today to speak about a very important change that must be made to the Constitution of the United States. Do not be worried that I might suggest a change to the Bill of Rights. These first ten **amendments** to the Constitution will forever stand unchanged as the base of a **democratic** government. The Bill of Rights protects freedom of religion, speech, press, assembly, and **petition**. These are our most important rights.

The Bill of Rights has other freedoms. It protects the basic rights of citizens relating to searches, just and fair punishment, and civil trials. No one would want to see citizens or states stripped of the rights they have that are not listed in the Constitution. We all agree that the bearing of arms for the protection of the country is important.

Yes, my fellow Americans, these ten and many of the other Amendments to the Constitution must hold down democracy. What I find we need is a change to the 12th Amendment and Article III, Section 2. These parts list rules on the election of the president. The problems these parts have created have ruined many presidential elections in history. They have stirred ill-feeling between political parties and party candidates even in our times.

To elect the president, the **Framers** of the Constitution set up a body of people, or **electors**. Today, we call this body the **Electoral College**. The electors are men and women who are supposed to be perfectly informed in politics. Article III, Section 2 of the Constitution states that "Each state shall appoint, in such manner as the **legislature** thereof may direct, a number of Electors, equal to the number of Senators and Representatives, to which the State may be entitled in the Congress; but no Senator or Representative, or person holding an office of trust or profit, under the United States, shall be appointed an Elector." Thus, each state gets two electors for its two senators and as many more electors as the state has members in the House of Representatives. The number of representatives, you remember, is based on the population of the state. The 12th Amendment explains how the votes for president and vice president will be made and taken. It tells what will happen if no one wins more than half of the votes.

When the Framers set up this strange system—voters vote for a candidate, then electors vote for the president—they had reasons. Many said that the common man—and it was definitely just men, and just white men at the time—did not have the political knowledge to pick a candidate. This is a point that no longer seems correct. Today, lots of information is available. With the impact of newspapers and computers, voters can learn as much as they want about the candidates. In fact, they can hardly miss learning! Nothing could possibly make en elector better able to choose the president than you or I. Nothing, I say.

Furthermore, the system doesn't work the way it was supposed to. At first the state legislatures selected electors. And maybe we could agree that the people in the legislature know more about politics than everyday men and women. But by the 1830s in almost every state, the electors were picked in the **popular election**. The electors, I say, NOT the candidates! Let me explain how this happens.

Voters like you go to the polls and in most states, you see a party team for president and vice president listed together. You cast your vote. But you are not exactly voting for the president and vice president. You are voting for their team of electors who will be in the Electoral College if they win. At the Electoral College meeting that takes place after the popular election, these electors should vote for the candidate you wanted. But, alas, they do not have to. No law says that electors cannot vote against the popular choice.

Completing a fact/opinion chart

Add to this fact/opinion chart by including more facts and opinions. Use one of the following focuses for your center box: *Bill of Rights* (paragraphs 1 and 2) or *History of the System* (paragraphs 5 and 6). You can copy whole sentences, parts of sentences to suggest the whole, or reword the statements.

FACTS		OPINIONS
Framers set up Electoral College. In the Constitution, Article III, Section 2 states . . . how number of electors determined number of representatives based on population The 12th Amendment explains . . .	**12th Amendment and Article III, Section 2**	What I find we need is a change to the 12th Amendment and Article III, Section 2. These rules have ruined many presidential elections and stirred ill-feeling between political parties and party candidates.

Read the second part of the argumentative speech "Let's Get Down to Democracy."

Now here's another problem. Each state, as you remember, has electors equal to the number of members it has in Congress (the Senate and the House of Representatives). So a large state has many electors, and a small state few. What happens when the popular vote in a large state is almost 50-50? The best thing would be for half the electors to vote for one candidate and half for the other. That would best reflect the popular vote. But the candidate with 51% of the vote gets all the electors. That is just not fair.

Are you beginning to see what happens with this Electoral College system? The votes of the electors never clearly represent the votes of the people. A president can win the most votes from citizens and still lose the election. In fact, this has happened four times. In 1824, Andrew Jackson had the most votes, 151,174, or 40.3% of the citizen's votes. John Quincy Adams had 113,122 votes, or 30.9%. Since Jackson did not have a clear **majority**, the issue went to the House, as stated in the 12th Amendment, who unfairly chose Adams. In 1876, Rutherford B. Hayes had 254,237 fewer votes than Samuel J. Tilden. But Hayes had 185 electoral votes, to Tilden's 184. It made a lot of voters angry to see their selected candidate lose. Then in 1888 President Grover Cleveland, running for re-election, won 90,596 more votes than Benjamin Harrison. But Harrison got an astounding 233 electoral votes, and Cleveland had just 168. Then in 2000, Al Gore won the popular vote but lost the Electoral College vote to George W. Bush.

Let's get back to the fact that electors don't have to vote the way the voters did. This is not just a theory. It has happened in numerous elections. Without a good reason, electors have changed sides after they were chosen. That is not a representative government, a democracy. It makes democracy look dumb!

The system also means, as I pointed out in the Jackson/Adams case, that the election of the president may eventually take place in the House of Representatives. Here, each state's representatives must decide together on the candidate and then cast only one vote per state. What does this have to do with the popular election? Why bother having one, if that's what's going to happen?

It is time now for a direct popular election of the President of the United States. Let's set aside all of these old and useless ways of electing our president, ways set up before education and information became common to the common people. The Constitution and even Amendments to it have been changed many times. Change is the way of democracy.

In a direct election, each voter gets one vote. Each individual vote would count equally in a direct election. This would be the most simple and easy solution to the Electoral College problem.

Smaller states might argue that this is unfair since in the Electoral College they have more than their share of representatives. Remember, all states, no matter how small, get at least two electors for their two senators. Are we one nation now or a bunch of jealous states? States that have a high population, a high number of voters, get more votes than states with a lower population. That is right and just. Opponents of the popular vote say that it weakens the states' powers. They ask what the point of having states is if states don't count in the presidential election. I say, let's go to the direct popular vote. Let's graduate from the Electoral College!

Using a fact/opinion chart

Fill in the fact/opinion chart for the second half of the argumentative speech. Consider using three of these focuses for your center boxes: *Large State Splits in Vote, Historical and Recent Occurrences, Problems with Elector Votes, Problems with House Votes, Direct Election.*

FACTS		OPINIONS

Check Your Understanding

Think about what you've read. Then answer these questions.

1. Which of these statements based on the argumentative speech cannot be proved?
   - Ⓐ No law says that electors cannot vote against the popular choice.
   - Ⓑ Voters go to the polls and see the president and vice president listed together.
   - Ⓒ When the Framers set up this system, they had reasons.
   - Ⓓ Without good reason, electors have changed sides after they were chosen.

2. Which word below is one of the words that signal the statement is an opinion? "We all agree that the bearing of arms for the protection of the country is important."
   - Ⓐ bearing
   - Ⓑ all
   - Ⓒ agree
   - Ⓓ protection

3. For presidential elections, what is meant by a "majority of votes"?
   - Ⓐ more than half of the total votes
   - Ⓑ more votes than another candidate
   - Ⓒ 50% of the votes
   - Ⓓ votes that hold more power

4. In this speech, Framers are
   - Ⓐ the people who built the electoral college.
   - Ⓑ the common voters.
   - Ⓒ the first president and vice president of the United States.
   - Ⓓ the men who debated and developed the Constitution.

5. Which word completes the analogy?
   legislature:senator::Electoral College:____
   - Ⓐ federalism
   - Ⓑ democratic
   - Ⓒ elector
   - Ⓓ petition

6. What is the main idea of the speech?
   - Ⓐ The electors do not know how to do their jobs.
   - Ⓑ The election of the president and vice president is important.
   - Ⓒ The electoral system should be replaced by a vote of the people.
   - Ⓓ The Framers of the Constitution did not realize how poor the Electoral College system would become.

7. In elections today, what normally happens after the voters' votes are counted?
   - Ⓐ Electors select the president.
   - Ⓑ The House of Representatives chooses the new president.
   - Ⓒ The popular election is held.
   - Ⓓ The Senate selects the president.

8. In the phrases "direct election" and "direct popular vote," what does the word *direct* mean?
   - Ⓐ "straight to the point"
   - Ⓑ "by action of the voters"
   - Ⓒ "not turning"
   - Ⓓ "using the exact words of the speaker"

9. What is the purpose of the speech?
   - Ⓐ to convince all voters to go to the polls
   - Ⓑ to demonstrate the poor character of most electors
   - Ⓒ to convince people to do away with the system of electors
   - Ⓓ to explain that the Constitution requires frequent changes

10. Why does the speaker get upset by the fact that a candidate who takes only 51% of the vote gets all the electors for the state?
   - Ⓐ Small states will have a greater say in the election.
   - Ⓑ Large states will determine who wins the election.
   - Ⓒ It does not reflect the choice of the voters.
   - Ⓓ It is not allowed in the Constitution.

11. How is election of the president by electors different from election of the president in the House of Representatives?

Ⓐ With electors, each state has a greater number of votes.

Ⓑ With electors, voters do not get to cast their ballots.

Ⓒ The electoral balloting takes place only after a legislative tie.

Ⓓ The electoral balloting represents the true wishes of the people.

12. What does the speaker mean by the phrase "graduate from the Electoral College"?

Ⓐ move beyond it to something better

Ⓑ hold a ceremony to end it

Ⓒ create more levels of government to control elections

Ⓓ make electors return to school to review politics

Extend Your Learning

- *Write Your Own Argumentative Speech*

  Research and write a short speech that supports the 12th Amendment and Article III, Section 2. Use a fact/opinion chart to organize the main points you will make and the facts and opinions you will use to support them. Present your finished speech to the class.

- *Fact/Opinion Game*

  In small groups, pick a topic everyone knows something about. Create a fact/opinion chart for your group and write three facts on the topic and three opinions. When you are finished, randomly present your facts and opinions to another group or to the class. Have the students identify which are the facts and which are the opinions.

- *Debate the Issues*

  As a class, select several issues of importance to your school, your community, or the nation. Set up sides for debating the issues. Plan the facts and opinions you will use to support your side in the debate. If possible and appropriate to your topic, bring in visuals (photographs, pictures, slides shows, etc.) for added evidence and interest.

Identifying Author's Purpose

Learn About Identifying Author's Purpose

Thinking about the strategy

Author's purpose is the reason an author has for writing. Every type of writing—essay, story, or poem, for example—has a purpose. Authors normally write for one of four main reasons. To identify the purpose, pay attention to the key details and ideas.

PURPOSE	WHAT THE AUTHOR PRESENTS
to describe	lots of vivid details that help the reader picture people, places, and things
to entertain	an interesting, enjoyable story, essay, or other type of writing
to persuade	an argument with reasons to convince the reader to think, believe, or act in a certain way
to explain/inform	factual information about a topic or a process

Once you determine the author's purpose, you can decide your own purpose for reading. For example, if the author's purpose is to persuade, your purpose for reading is to decide if you agree with the author.

Studying a model

Read the first part of the letter and the notes beside it.

100 Visitors Way
Picture City, IL 66666
July 10, 2005

At the start, it is hard to tell the author's main purpose.

The second sentence tries to persuade.

The third sentence explains what is at the museum.

"Our biggest adventure" sounds like the beginning of an entertaining story.

The scene of the trees at lunch is very descriptive.

Dear Aunt Julia,
    We visited the museum as you suggested. You must visit it yourself! The museum has hundreds of famous paintings, four rooms of photographs, and displays that put you into the middle of different kinds of landforms and habitats. But our biggest adventure happened at lunch! Mother, Estéban, and I picked a table in the courtyard. Blossoming trees, in shades of icy pink and cool lavender, dropped soft petals on us as we sipped refreshing water and waited for our lunches. Soon the waiter, dressed in crisp white, delivered delicious-smelling, fresh hot rolls.

Learn About a Graphic Organizer

Understanding an author's purpose questionnaire

An **author's purpose questionnaire** helps you sort out the ideas, information, facts, and details in a reading selection.

You will notice how an author often uses a combination of purposes in a selection, but focuses on one purpose as the main purpose.

Here is an author's purpose questionnaire for the letter on page 94.

QUESTION: Why does the author . . .	PURPOSE
say, "You must visit it yourself"?	to persuade the reader of the letter to go to the museum
tell what is at the museum?	to impress the reader with the types of displays
say, "But our biggest adventure happened at lunch"?	to suggest that an entertaining story may follow
tell about the trees in the courtyard?	to describe the scene where the adventure took place

The author's purpose questionnaire lays out the purposes of different ideas and details in the writing. You begin to focus on the purpose that seems most important to the author and to understand and evaluate how the author is affecting you.

Which purpose is most likely the author's main purpose?
The main purpose is probably to entertain, because the author says "biggest adventure" and then goes on to set the scene.

As you read, ask yourself

- Do descriptive words and images paint a picture for the reader? The main purpose may be to describe.
- Does the author relate a story or something else that is interesting? The main purpose may be to entertain and perhaps also to teach a lesson.
- Does the author state an opinion and support it with facts and reasons that convince you to do, buy, or believe something? The main purpose may be to persuade.
- Do many specific facts and details explain the steps in a process or inform the reader about an idea, a plan, an object, and so on? The main purpose may be to explain or inform.

Learn About a Form of Writing

Focusing on a letter

A **letter** is written from one person to another. Friendly letters are usually personal. The most important part of a friendly letter is the body, where the writer expresses friendship and shares experiences. Business letters convey information clearly and efficiently. They may be written to order an item, request information, complain about a problem, or apply for a position.

Look for these characteristics of a letter.

- A letter can be a friendly or a business correspondence.
- A letter is written in a special form. A friendly letter has a heading, greeting, body, closing, and signature. A business letter adds an inside address after the heading.
- The purpose of a letter may be to inform, entertain, describe, or persuade.

Organizing ideas in an author's purpose questionnaire

Read the second part of the letter that begins on page 94. Then look at the author's purpose questionnaire.

> We relaxed as we chatted about the displays we had seen. Estéban took out his museum map and laid it on the table. "I'd like to visit this display. It puts you right into a temperate forest, animals and all." Well, the instant he finished his sentence, a small red squirrel leaped, or fell, from a branch above us onto the middle of the map. It scurried over to Estéban's bread plate, grabbed his roll, and disappeared with it into the trees! I can't say whose face looked funnier—Estéban's or the squirrel's. Anyway, we felt Estéban got a good taste of forest life and the squirrel got a good taste of Estéban's lunch! You'll have to go eat in the courtyard. You'll see what can happen there!
>
> Love,
> Juanita

QUESTION: Why does the author . . .	PURPOSE
tell what the map shows?	to inform the reader of the forest display to make the story funnier
tell about the squirrel?	to entertain the reader with an amusing series of events
say, "You'll have to go eat in the courtyard"?	to persuade the reader to eat there to risk having the same funny experience

The author includes explanation and persuasion to back up the amusing story. An author's purpose questionnaire helps you see how these different purposes support the main purpose—to entertain.

Prepare for the Reading Selections

Gaining knowledge

Art museums house collections of past and present drawings, writings, and statues. They often display pottery, jewelry, furniture, tools, ships, and musical instruments. Some museums exhibit full-sized architectural items such as tombs with mummies, cathedrals, temples, homes, and totem poles as well as replicas that help visitors imagine what certain places were like.

Yet when most people visit art museums, they expect to see paintings collected there, especially the paintings by recognized artists. Some of the names of these artists may be familiar. Rembrandt painted detailed and realistic portraits and still-life scenes in the 1600s. Claude Monet, in the 1870s, began a style of painting known as impressionism. Impressionists did not try to copy nature but focused on light and shadow to present their own "impression." Vincent Van Gogh and Mary Cassatt experimented with impressionism in the late 1800s. Paul Cezanne concentrated on capturing colors in Dutch landscapes. Piet Mondrian was an early 1900s artist who painted geometric designs. In the 1900s, Andrew Wyeth painted vast, sometimes lonely, rural scenes. On the following pages, you will read some letters that tell about visits to art museums.

Learn Vocabulary

Understanding vocabulary

The boxed words below are **boldfaced** in the selections. Learn the meaning of each word. Then write the word that completes the sentence.

critique
intricacy
subtle
nebulous
aromatic
appetizers
perspective
ultimate
hieroglyphics

1. The _____ in the drawing made the mountain look miles away.

2. I love the smell of _____ cedar.

3. These ancient Egyptian _____ tell the pharaoh's story.

4. If you eat too many _____ , you won't have room for dinner.

5. The _____ of this maze makes it hard to get from start to finish.

6. Always kind, Kelly's behavior is the _____ in courtesy.

7. Your _____ of the painting did not comment on the dull colors.

8. This light pink is barely noticeable, or _____ .

9. The forest is so dark, the trees are a _____ mass of trunks and branches.

Read the first two letters about visits to art museums.

6 Mirrabelle Lane
Sugarhill, CA 99999
September 2, 2005

Dear Abdul,

I really wish you had come to the Herald Art Museum with me last Sunday. The gray stone building wraps like a snake around a huge tree-decorated courtyard. Inside the courtyard is a flower-filled, sweet smelling English garden. Just entering through the massive carved doors seemed magical. But now I've experienced the exhibits. I've seen what there is to see (or rather, begun to see, since the museum is mammoth). I know that you will have to visit it with me next time.

The Herald is an incredible museum. It must be the best in the world! Consider this feature. You can walk an art history timeline. It begins 30,000 years ago and takes you right up to the present. I doubt any other museum in the country or the world does that! Along the timeline, you find precisely copied replicas or original artwork (of course, they explain which is which). You start at cave art, move to Greek vases, to Rembrandt, to painters who are still developing their skills today. Rembrandt's portraits, with their dark backgrounds and somber figures, look real. You can practically touch the pearls hanging around the lady's neck or pet the fluffy dog.

Secondly, the museum has a masters' exhibit. It is not just one or two rooms like other museums I've been to, but a whole wing of paintings by the greatest artists in history. The exhibit includes 25 paintings by Claude Monet, 33 by Mary Cassatt, 45 by Vincent Van Gogh, and 15 by Paul Cezanne, to name just a few. Everyone who is interested in art, the way we are, should study all these works.

Last month, *Museum Magazine* presented a **critique** of the Herald. Guess what they said? "If you can go only to one art museum, take in this one—it's one in a million." Have I convinced you? I hope so.

Your friend,
Alexander

1234 Whisper Boulevard
New York, New York 22222
August 22, 2005

Dear Augusta,

I just returned from the Museum of Art where a Monet exhibit is in progress. This was the first time I saw his work close up. I studied about 25 versions of the Rouen Cathedral in France. Monet painted these in the late 1800s to show different times of day, sunrise to sunset. What I found remarkable is the **intricacy** of shapes and shadows dancing on the canvas. The colors in my favorite were **subtle** shades of grey, brown, tan, gold, and blue. The paint was layered thickly, so that when I approached close, all I could see were blobs, dots, and strokes of oozy paint. But as I stepped back, as if magically, the huge cathedral emerged in **nebulous** yet perfect detail. You must see this for yourself to believe it!

Yours truly,
Michelle

Completing an author's purpose questionnaire

Some of the author's purpose questionnaire has been filled in. Finish the questionnaire with information about the purpose of ideas and/or details in the two letters.

QUESTION: Why does the author . . .	PURPOSE
	to persuade the reader of how great the Herald Art Museum is
list the number of paintings by certain artists at the Herald Art Museum? quote *Museum Magazine?*	
	to help the reader picture the paintings by Monet at the Museum of Art

Read the next two letters about visits to art museums.

1 Elderberry Lane
Cliffside, NM 56789
July 13, 2005

Dear Helena,

I was absolutely amazed by Markland Museum. You'll want to go there. We set off very early Tuesday. We rode past rust-colored mountains and craggy rocks, **aromatic** forests, and fields of tiny pink wildflowers. These scenes were **appetizers** to the main course!

You wouldn't believe all the art at the museum. Yet what mostly impressed me is what I learned about painting. Did you know that color, line, mass, space, texture, composition, and light and shade are the qualities that make up paintings? Do you even know what all these terms mean? (I didn't.) So I'll tell you!

Color is simple. It is the hues and shades the painter uses. Yet color can do so much. It can make a painting cheerful, like yellow sunflowers on a Van Gogh canvas. Color echoes nature or extends it. It suggests time of year or time of day.

Line is the shapes and forms the painter uses. Sometimes line copies the natural objects. Sometimes it adds **perspective**. Sometimes, like in a Mondrian painting, line is a major feature.

Mass is how much weight or fullness the painting seems to have. When you look at the mass, you consider how real the mountains seem, how heavy the rock appears, how solid the person is in the painting.

Do you know how an artist can make a painting look real? The artist uses space. Space is how the lines, colors, and mass work together to make the viewer believe that the painting is more than a flat surface. Space also conveys feelings. The open space in Andrew Wyeth's painting *Teel's Island* made me feel very lonely.

I love texture. Think about the deep ridges and valleys of thick paint on a Van Gogh. Thick brushstrokes outline circles of stars on his *Starry, Starry Night*.

Every painting has composition. This is the way the parts are arranged. Chinese landscapes set the elements in a way that draws you into the magic of the painting. That's really wonderful.

Oh, I almost forgot light and shade—how these attract your eye to certain parts of a painting. They also accent the scene or create space, and change colors. Look at paintings by Monet to see the **ultimate** in light and shade!

I hope you like my "lesson" about painting. Write soon.

Your good friend,
Kyle

2200 1st 23rd Street, Building A
Gonzales, TX 89898
October 11, 2005

Grandma Harriet,

   You wouldn't believe what happened at the Hill Museum. We were in the Egyptian room. Little Jonathan (you know how inquisitive he is) kept asking questions about the looming statues and carved stone walls of ancient **hieroglyphics**. I tried to read about each display to answer his questions. Before I could finish, he'd run off to the next. Once he raced down a long, dark corridor to a mummy case. Before I could reach him, he scurried back startled yet grinning. "What happened?" I asked. He explained that he had asked a question and the mummy had answered. Then it had warned him not to stray too far from his family. I glanced over and a museum guard near the mummy case winked at me. I didn't explain this to Jonathan, and he stayed by my side the rest of the day!

                                        Love,
                                        Your Grandson Matt

Using an author's purpose questionnaire   Fill in the author's purpose questionnaire with your thoughts about author's purpose in the second pair of letters.

QUESTION: Why does the author . . .	PURPOSE

101

Check Your Understanding

Think about what you've read. Then answer these questions.

1. The main purpose of Alexander's letter to Abdul is
   - Ⓐ to entertain Abdul with an interesting story.
   - Ⓑ to explain how art has changed over time.
   - Ⓒ to describe Rembrandt's works.
   - Ⓓ to persuade Abdul to go to the Herald Art Museum.

2. Kyle's letter to Helena mainly
   - Ⓐ describes the colors in paintings.
   - Ⓑ offers opinions about certain artists.
   - Ⓒ presents an entertaining story.
   - Ⓓ explains elements that make up paintings.

3. A subtle compliment is one that is
   - Ⓐ not very sincere.
   - Ⓑ obvious.
   - Ⓒ barely noticeable.
   - Ⓓ honest.

4. Which word completes the analogy?
   appetizers:food::hieroglyphics:_____
   - Ⓐ subtle
   - Ⓑ writing
   - Ⓒ perspective
   - Ⓓ ancient

5. Which sentence is the best summary of Grandson Matt's letter to Grandma Harriet?
   - Ⓐ Matt tries to keep up with his little brother in the museum until a guard tricks Jonathan, making Matt's task easier.
   - Ⓑ Jonathan tries to annoy his older brother by asking him lots of questions and then running off.
   - Ⓒ A museum guard shows a young visitor a mummy that talks.
   - Ⓓ A visit to a museum turns into a scary experience for a young boy and his brother.

6. A painting with nebulous perspective would
   - Ⓐ indicate distance clearly.
   - Ⓑ show depth only vaguely.
   - Ⓒ include lots of empty space.
   - Ⓓ present a cloudy scene.

7. Which of these is the main idea of Kyle's letter to Helena?
   - Ⓐ Everyone should study the paintings of Van Gogh.
   - Ⓑ Funny things can happen at a museum.
   - Ⓒ Paintings consist of certain elements that can be used in different ways.
   - Ⓓ To really understand art, a person must read about the artists and their work.

8. According to Kyle, thick paint on a canvas gives the painting
   - Ⓐ line.
   - Ⓑ color.
   - Ⓒ texture.
   - Ⓓ space.

9. Look at Michelle's letter to Augusta. What quality of Monet's paintings most impressed Michelle?
   - Ⓐ Monet used many colors.
   - Ⓑ The detailed paintings can look like nothing close up.
   - Ⓒ An 1800s painter created these scenes.
   - Ⓓ The Rouen Cathedral was huge.

10. Alexander mentions a "masters' exhibit" in the next to last paragraph of his letter. In this sentence, a master is
    - Ⓐ a person who owns something.
    - Ⓑ someone who controls another person.
    - Ⓒ the captain of a merchant ship.
    - Ⓓ someone especially skilled at something.

11. Which sentence from Alexander's letter to Abdul is not an opinion?

Ⓐ Last month, *Museum Magazine* presented a critique of the Herald.

Ⓑ "If you can go only to one art museum, take in this one—it's one in a million."

Ⓒ The Herald is an incredible museum.

Ⓓ Everyone who is interested in art, the way we are, should study all these works.

12. What is the figure of speech in this sentence from Alexander's letter?

The gray stone building wraps like a snake around a huge tree-decorated courtyard.

Ⓐ a personification that gives the building the human ability to wrap gifts

Ⓑ a simile comparing the building to a snake

Ⓒ a metaphor comparing the courtyard to a forest

Ⓓ a simile comparing trees to decorations

Extend Your Learning

- *A Purposeful Letter*

  Write a four-paragraph letter. For your topic, pick a museum you have visited, a play you have attended, or a piece of art you have seen. Or find a picture of a painting, sculpture, statue, etc. you especially like. Describe something in the first paragraph, tell a story about your topic in the second, explain something in the third, and persuade your reader to believe, think, or do something in the fourth.

- *Real-life Purposes*

  Find an example of a letter, such as a business correspondence, a newspaper letter to the editor, a child's letter in *Cobblestone* or another children's magazine, or a personal letter you are willing to share. Use an author's purpose questionnaire to study how purposes blend in the letter and determine the main purpose.

- *Room # ___'s Museum*

  Work with a group to plan what you would put in a museum to show something about life and art in your classroom. Draw your plans on paper and/or set up a real display of artwork, objects, tools, furniture, and so on. Invite other classes to view your museum.

Interpreting Figurative Language

Learn About Interpreting Figurative Language

Thinking about the strategy

When you look up a word in the dictionary, you find its literal meaning. The literal meaning is the definition. Yet authors often use words in another way, a figurative way. **Figurative language** creates a picture or an image with words that are used in ways that reach beyond their usual meanings.

Figurative Language		Example	Explanation
A simile	makes a comparison using the word *like* or *as*.	That beetle is as big as a three-stage rocket.	Compares two unlike things based on a similar quality, bigness.
A metaphor	makes a comparison without the word *like* or *as*, using a direct statement that says one thing is another.	The jay is a whizzing airplane.	Compares two unlike things that are similar in one way, the speed of an airplane and a jay.
Personification	makes a comparison by giving something that is not human the traits of a human. (Personification is a special type of metaphor.)	The wind grabbed my hat.	Something that is not human, the wind, is given the human ability to take hold of a hat.

To find figurative language in a reading selection, look for words used in surprising ways and images made fresh by unique comparisons.

Studying a model

Read the paragraph and the notes beside it.

Shoots are given the human ability to peek—a personification.

With as, the warmth of the soil is compared to the sun—a simile.

A third shoot calls out the way people do—a personification.

The garden with all its shoots is said to be an army—a metaphor.

"Earlier than last year" is a comparison but it is literal, not figurative.

Springtime

Tiny green shoots peeked through the rain-dampened ground. The soil was now as warm as the spring sun. First, I noticed one shoot, then two. Then a third called to me, "I'm here! Look here!" As I gazed at the whole field, the garden transformed into a fine army dressed in new green. Springtime had arrived, earlier than last year.

Learn About a Graphic Organizer

Understanding a figurative language chart

To appreciate a story or a poem that uses figurative language, you need to be aware of and understand the comparisons. A **figurative language chart** allows you to note figurative comparisons and examine each one to determine what the author wants you to see, hear, or experience. Taken all together, the figurative comparisons help you better understand the reading selection.

Here is a figurative language chart for the paragraph on page 104.

Comparison	What Is Compared	What It Means/Suggests
"Tiny green shoots peeked through the rain-dampened ground." (personification)	green shoots/person peeking	Green shoots were barely appearing, sort of secretly.
"The soil was now as warm as the spring sun." (simile)	soil/spring sun	Soil was pleasantly warm and comforting.
"Then a third called to me, 'I'm here! Look here!'" (personification)	shoot/person calling	A shoot drew the author's attention, gently but commandingly.
"As I gazed at the whole field, the garden transformed into a fine army dressed in new green." (metaphor)	garden/army	Shoots are plentiful, orderly, and strong.

Understanding figurative language helps you avoid misunderstanding the author. You know that the author does not mean the shoots turned into a real army— only that they are similar to an army in their abundance, organization, and strength.

As you read, ask yourself

- Does the author use similes, metaphors, and/or personification?
- What two unlike things are compared? In what way are they alike?
- What unique images are created by the figurative language? What do they add to your understanding of the selection?

Learn About a Form of Writing

Focusing on poetry You usually recognize that writing is **poetry** by looking at the way the words appear on a page. Poetry is normally set in lines or groups of lines (stanzas) rather than in paragraphs. But no one has an exact definition of poetry. Scholars say that poetry is writing that is imaginative and intense, that goes beyond mere words to the inner impact of these words on the reader. Though there are many types of poems—from ballads to haiku, from lyrics to sonnets, from epics to free verse—at the heart of all poetry is emotion, thought, and image meant to affect you, the reader: to make you see, feel, or think about things in a different way.

Poetry has certain characteristics of form that help you distinguish it from other writing.

- Poetry has a regular rhythm, or meter, that emerges from the accented syllables in the words.
- Poetry may use rhyme—words that sound alike, such as *tree/bee*.
- Poetry uses figurative language and concrete images to appeal to the senses and the feelings of the reader.

Organizing ideas in a figurative language chart Read the poem by Alfred, Lord Tennyson and study the figurative language chart.

The Eagle: A Fragment

He clasps the crag with crooked hands;
Close to the sun in lonely lands,
Ringed with the azure world, he stands.
The wrinkled sea beneath him crawls;
He watches from his mountain walls,
And like a thunderbolt, he falls.

Comparison	What Is Compared	What It Means/Suggests
"He clasps the crag with crooked hands;" (personification)	eagle's claws/person's hands	The eagle is humanlike, powerful, perhaps old and wise.
"The wrinkled sea beneath him crawls;" (metaphor/ personification)	sea/something wrinkled sea/person crawling	The sea's surface is wavy. The sea seems to advance slowly, creeping.
"He watches from his mountain walls," (metaphor)	mountain/the walls of a building	The mountain is tall, like a fortified castle that the eagle owns.
"And like a thunderbolt, he falls." (simile)	how the eagle dives/ a thunderbolt	The eagle's dive is like lightning, extremely fast and powerful.

106

Prepare for the Reading Selections

Gaining knowledge

Poetry is like a puzzle: until you examine the pieces and put them together to experience the picture, you may not grasp the meaning. The poems you will read on the pages that follow comment on nature. Here are facts about each poem—puzzle pieces—to help you assemble their meaning.

"Rhodora: On Being Asked, Whence is the Flower?" by Ralph Waldo Emerson was published in 1839. The flowers of the rhodora, or rhododendron bush, appear before the leaves. The bush Emerson describes grows in the deserted woods. In the title, the word *whence* means "from where." The word *solitudes* in the first line is usually singular: you know that *solitude* suggests aloneness or quiet thought.

In "I Wandered Lonely As a Cloud," William Wordsworth describes his sighting, in 1802, of a field of daffodils. In the last stanza, Wordsworth reveals a later effect of this experience. The word *o'er*, in the second line, is a contraction for *over*.

In the first stanza of "Ode to the West Wind," published in 1820, Percy Bysshe Shelley describes the autumn wind's force and hints at spring. *Thou* means "you" and *thine* is a formal (considered poetic at the time) word for *your*. The order in many of the sentences is unusual, but if you read carefully and pay attention to the punctuation, you can figure out the meaning.

Learn Vocabulary

Understanding vocabulary

The boxed words below are **boldfaced** in the selections. Learn the meaning of each word. Then write the word that could replace the underlined word(s) in the sentence.

nook
array
vales
jocund
pensive
hectic
pestilence
multitudes
clarion
preserver

1. _____ The <u>medieval trumpet</u> announced the king.

2. _____ The Black Death was a <u>deadly disease</u>.

3. _____ A flower grew in the <u>hidden spot</u>.

4. _____ Her life is so <u>feverishly busy</u> she rarely rests.

5. _____ <u>Huge numbers</u> of insects buzzed around me.

6. _____ The <u>splendid attire</u> of the general dazzled us.

7. _____ Soft winds brushed the hills and <u>valleys</u>.

8. _____ Caring for all, he was a <u>guardian</u> of life.

9. _____ The <u>cheerful</u> clerk always smiled.

10. _____ I feel very <u>sad and thoughtful</u> today.

Reading Selection—Part One

Read the poem "The Rhodora: On Being Asked, Whence is the Flower?" by Ralph Waldo Emerson.

The Rhodora: On Being Asked, Whence is the Flower?

In May, when sea-winds pierced our solitudes,
I found the fresh Rhodora in the woods,
Spreading its leafless blooms in a damp **nook**,
To please the desert and the sluggish brook.
The purple petals, fallen in the pool,
Made the black water with their beauty gay;
Here might the red-bird come his plumes to cool,
And court the flower that cheapens his **array**.
Rhodora! If the sages ask you why,
This charm is wasted on the earth and sky,
Tell them, dear, that if eyes were made for seeing,
Then Beauty is its own excuse for being:
Why you were there, O rival of the rose!
I never thought to ask, I never knew;
But, in my simple ignorance, suppose
The self-same Power that brought me there brought you.

Ralph Waldo Emerson

Completing a figurative language chart

Some of the figurative language chart for the poem above has been filled in. Add the missing parts.

Comparison	What Is Compared	What It Means/Suggests
In May, when sea-winds pierced our solitudes (metaphor)	sea-winds/something that can pierce, like a sword	
(personification/metaphor)	flower/person spreading something, pleasing someone woods/desert	The plant drops its flowers to please the forest, to spread its beauty on purpose. The woods are like a desert, not dry but empty, deserted.

Read the poems "I Wandered Lonely As a Cloud" by William Wordsworth and "Ode to the West Wind, Stanza I" by Percy Bysshe Shelley.

I Wandered Lonely As a Cloud

I wandered lonely as a cloud
That floats on high o'er **vales** and hills,
When all at once I saw a crowd,
A host, of golden daffodils;
Beside the lake, beneath the trees,
Fluttering and dancing in the breeze.

Continuous as the stars that shine
And twinkle on the milky way,
They stretched in never-ending line
Along the margin of a bay:
Ten thousand saw I at a glance,
Tossing their heads in sprightly dance.

The waves beside them danced; but they
Outdid the sparkling waves in glee;
A poet could not but be gay,
In such a **jocund** company;
I gazed—and gazed—but little thought
What wealth the show to me had brought:

For oft, when on my couch I lie
In vacant or in **pensive** mood,
They flash upon that inward eye
Which is the bliss of solitude;
And then my heart with pleasure fills,
And dances with the daffodils.

William Wordsworth

Ode to the West Wind, Stanza I

O wild West Wind, thou breath of Autumn's being,
Thou, from whose unseen presence the leaves dead
Are driven, like ghosts from an enchanter fleeing,

Yellow, and black, and pale, and **hectic** red,
Pestilence-stricken **multitudes**: O thou,
Who did chariot to their dark wintry bed

The winged seeds, where they lie cold and low,
Each like a corpse within its grave, until
Thine azure sister of the Spring shall blow

Her **clarion** o'er the dreaming earth, and fill
(Driving sweet buds like flocks to feed in air)
With living hues and odors plain and hill:

Wild Spirit, which art moving everywhere;
Destroyer and **preserver**; hear, oh hear!

Percy Bysshe Shelley

*Using a figurative
language chart*

Find examples of figurative language (similes, metaphors, personification) in the poems in Part Two. Fill in the figurative language chart to list and explain your examples. You can use a separate piece of paper if you need more room.

Comparison	What Is Compared	What It Means/Suggests

111

Check Your Understanding

Think about what you've read. Then answer these questions.

1. Which of these lines from the second and third stanzas of "I Wandered Lonely As a Cloud" does not contain figurative language?
   Ⓐ Ten thousand saw I at a glance,
   Ⓑ Tossing their heads in sprightly dance.
   Ⓒ The waves beside them danced; but they
   Ⓓ Outdid the sparkling waves in glee;

2. What is compared in this line from "Ode to the West Wind"?
   "Driving sweet buds like flocks to feed in air"
   Ⓐ the wind and the air
   Ⓑ budding plants and groups of grazing animals
   Ⓒ cars and flocks of animals
   Ⓓ buds and people who feed livestock

3. What would you most likely find in a nook?
   Ⓐ multitudes of athletes
   Ⓑ a pestilence
   Ⓒ a pensive poet
   Ⓓ hills and vales

4. The array of a bird would be its
   Ⓐ wings.   Ⓒ flight.
   Ⓑ tail.   Ⓓ feathers.

5. Which word names a musical instrument?
   Ⓐ clarion   Ⓒ jocund
   Ⓑ preserver   Ⓓ pestilence

6. From "The Rhodora: On Being Asked, Whence is the Flower?", which of these best restates the following line about the red-bird?
   "And court the flower that cheapens his array."
   Ⓐ Take the flower before a judge to prove that it is more beautiful than the bird.
   Ⓑ Make the flower go to a formal meeting because it spoils too quickly.
   Ⓒ Love the flower by stealing its beauty.
   Ⓓ Visit the flower that makes the bird look less elegant.

7. In "The Rhodora: On Being Asked, Whence is the Flower?" what do the purple petals do?
   Ⓐ turn the water black
   Ⓑ interest the sages
   Ⓒ color the water cheerfully
   Ⓓ sink under the black water

8. In "The Rhodora: On Being Asked, Whence is the Flower?", what main idea does Emerson suggest?
   Ⓐ It doesn't matter where the flower is as long as it grows well and birds enjoy it.
   Ⓑ The flower is where it belongs, as we all are.
   Ⓒ The beauty of the flower is wasted where it grows.
   Ⓓ Like all things, flowers decay, and the petals fall into brooks or onto the ground.

9. Which of these is the best summary of "I Wandered Lonely As a Cloud"?
   Ⓐ The poet walks along the water until he comes to a garden of daffodils. He stops to admire it.
   Ⓑ The wandering poet comes upon daffodils blown by the wind. This remembered scene still makes him happy.
   Ⓒ The poet wanders into a field of flowers that remind him of the milky way. He describes the beauty of the galaxy.
   Ⓓ The poet feels like a cloud as he dances in a field of daffodils. Then he goes home to rest on his couch.

10. Which line from the last stanza of "I Wandered Lonely As a Cloud" suggests an opinion?
   Ⓐ For oft, when on my couch I lie
   Ⓑ In vacant or in pensive mood,
   Ⓒ They flash upon that inward eye
   Ⓓ Which is the bliss of solitude;

11. The rest of Shelley's poem "Ode to the West Wind" most likely

  Ⓐ tells what the poet does in autumn.

  Ⓑ describes other effects of the west wind.

  Ⓒ discusses other winds, such as the north wind and the south wind.

  Ⓓ explains what animals do in autumn and why.

12. What similar idea makes all three poems alike?

  Ⓐ an appreciation of nature and natural forces

  Ⓑ a fear of stormy weather and winds

  Ⓒ a belief that nature reflects the life of people

  Ⓓ a dislike of human interference in nature

Extend Your Learning

• *Write a Poem*

  Think of something in nature that you find pleasing, inspiring, frightening, or disgusting. Write a poem to get your feeling across to your readers. Draw a picture, paint a scene, or find/take a photograph to accompany your poem. Post your visual and your poem on a bulletin board.

• *Wake Up Worn-out Images*

  Some comparisons have been so overused that they no longer create a fresh and exciting image: *as hungry as a wolf, as big as a house.* Work with a group to think of or research these expressions. (You may find examples listed as clichés and/or idioms.) Then for each worn-out image or expression, create a new figurative comparison that is more powerful than the overused expression: *as hungry as a shipwrecked sailor, as big as a hot-air balloon.*

• *Read Poetry*

  Get a poetry anthology from the classroom or library and skim some of the poems until you find ones that interest you. After you have read several poems, use a figurative language chart to study the two or three poems you like best. Do the poems use figurative language heavily or lightly? Do the poems you selected have any similarities in language? Form? Content? Share one poem orally with a group and explain one of its figurative comparisons.

Summarizing

Learn About Summarizing

*Thinking about
the strategy*

A **summary** is a retelling of a book, a story, an article, or other work of fiction or nonfiction, in a shorter form. To summarize, readers must be able to identify key ideas in the text and then present those ideas in their own words and in a condensed form, without changing the basic meaning of the text. As a result, summarizing is an excellent way for readers to check their understanding of a reading selection.

To summarize a short story or other work of fiction, identify the main story elements, and then explain what happens. The main story elements are the setting, characters, and plot. When you are summarizing fiction, leave out unimportant details that do not affect the outcome of the story.

When you summarize nonfiction, you tell what the work is mainly about. To do this, identify the topic and then tell the key points that the author makes about the topic. One way to identify the key points is to answer the questions *Who? What? When? Where?* and *Why?* When you are summarizing nonfiction, leave out minor facts and details that do not help explain the main idea.

Studying a model

Read the passage from a nonfiction article and the notes beside it.

The first paragraph identifies the topic: eating well-balanced meals.

It tells who: school-age kids

It tells what: hamburgers, tacos, fries, and pizza.

It tells when: today; the present

Where: America

Why: too busy to eat well

Have you ever heard the saying, "You are what you eat"? For many young people, whose after-school schedule may include a combination of such things as homework, chores, sports practice and music lessons, games and recitals, doctor's appointments, and odd jobs, eating is an afterthought. Most parents try to provide balanced meals, but when no one is there to eat them, what's the point? If you are what you eat, then many American kids today are hamburgers, tacos, fries, and pizza.

In 2005, The United States Department of Agriculture created the new My Pyramid eating plan. The pyramid itself is a graphic outline of the guidelines for maintaining a nutritious diet. The pyramid is divided into vertical stripes. Each colored stripe represents a different food group. From left to right, orange is for grains. Green is for vegetables. Red is for fruits. Yellow is for fats and oils. Blue is for dairy and calcium-rich foods. Purple is for proteins, which include meats, beans, and fish. The width of the stripe suggests where the bulk of your diet should come from. On My Pyramid, the widest stripe is orange and narrowest stripe is yellow.

Learn About a Graphic Organizer

Understanding a 5Ws web

To identify the topic and main idea of a nonfiction selection, create a 5Ws web. A 5Ws web shows the important facts and details that the author uses to explain the topic.

This 5Ws web shows the topic and key points for the first paragraph of the passage on page 114.

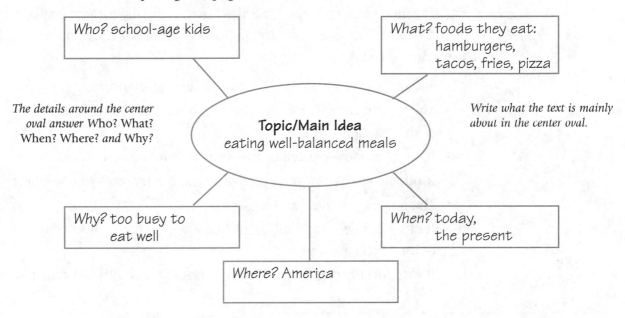

The details around the center oval answer Who? What? When? Where? and Why?

Write what the text is mainly about in the center oval.

You can use the details in a 5Ws web to write a summary of a passage or of an entire article. This example one-sentence summary of the first paragraph on page 114 is much shorter than the original:

Many American kids are so busy with after-school activities that they fail to eat well-balanced meals.

As you read, ask yourself

- What is the topic?
- What facts and details help explain the topic?
- What main idea does the author want me to understand about the topic?

Learn About a Form of Writing

*Focusing on
a magazine article*
What makes you want to read a magazine article? Is it because you're interested in the topic? Is it because of the catchy title? Is it because of the photographs, illustrations, and other visuals that illustrate the article? It's probably a combination of all these points.

A **magazine article** presents facts and details about a high-interest topic. The format of many magazine articles, which usually include heads, subheads, and illustrations, allows readers to preview the article to see if the topic is of interest to them.

A magazine article has these distinguishing characteristics.

- The topic is usually current and of high interest to a majority of the reading audience.
- It contains facts and details that help explain the main idea.
- It often contains statistics, examples, and quotations by knowledgeable people.
- The language is lively and engaging.
- It often has heads and subheads that suggest what each section of the article is about.
- It may include photographs, maps, diagrams, and other visual aids.

*Organizing ideas
in a 5Ws web*
You can use a 5Ws web to organize the key facts and details in a magazine article to create a summary. The 5Ws web below contains important details from the second paragraph of the passage on page 114. Keep in mind, that as you complete a 5Ws web for a passage, you may not find details that answer every W question. Be as thorough as you can be so that you can write a good summary.

Who? United States
Department
of Agriculture

What? pyramid that is
graphic outline for
a nutritious diet

Topic/Main Idea
My Pyramid Eating Plan

Why? to help people understand
which food groups to eat
the most of

When? 2005

Where? United States

Prepare for the Reading Selection

Gaining knowledge

At the professional sports level, contracts worth millions of dollars drive athletes to prove that they are worthy of the money and the adoration of their fans. Often these athletes play until their bodies give out. They have committed their lives to the sport.

On the following pages, you will read a magazine article about kids and sports. There is a great deal of controversy related to the participation of children in organized sports programs. Some doctors and athletic experts believe that children begin to specialize in one sport at too young an age. These children often don't have an opportunity to experience the fun associated with other sports. There are some experts who also feel that children, as young as four and five years old, are pushed too hard to commit to and excel at a sport. This is too great an expectation for such little kids. After all, you don't expect ordinary first graders to be reading Shakespeare or doing algebra.

Learn Vocabulary

Understanding vocabulary

The boxed words below are **boldfaced** in the selection. Learn the meaning of each word. Then write the word beside its definition.

pummeled
unrealistic
adept
exhilaration
motivator
renowned
outweigh
psychological
alternative
socialize

1. _____ well known as an expert at a particular skill

2. _____ not the way things are likely to happen in ordinary life

3. _____ a different choice

4. _____ to have more meaning; to be more important than

5. _____ the factor that pushes someone to do something

6. _____ repeatedly struck by someone

7. _____ extreme cheerfulness; extreme energy

8. _____ to be among other people; to meet with people

9. _____ skilled at doing something; talented

10. _____ having to do with the way the mind and brain work

Read the first part of the magazine article "Playing for the Fun of It."

Playing for the Fun of It

What do a ten-year-old baseball player and a 36-year-old professional football player have in common besides the fact that they play a sport?

Nothing, right? Actually, there may be one thing that the two share. It's possible that both the little leaguer and the pro have had enough of sports to last a lifetime.

You may find this difficult to fathom. After all, it's understandable that a 36-year-old football player, whose body has been battered and **pummeled** by 300-pound opponents for years, would be ready for retirement. However, isn't ten years old a little young to be thinking of hanging up the cleats?

To understand why, at ten, a kid might be ready to quit sports, you have to understand the highly competitive nature of youth sports in today's world.

The Spirit of Competition

Competition is supposed to be a good thing. Competition, at its best, forces us to push ourselves to excel, to reach deep within ourselves to find that very last ounce of effort and to use it. Learning to win and learning to lose are important life lessons. If we learn those lessons on the soccer field, in the swimming pool, at the ice rink, or on the basketball court while we're having fun, then that's a great learning experience.

But are kids actually having fun playing sports?

According to a 2004 article on MSNBC.com, approximately 30 million kids in elementary and high school participate in organized sports. Many experts in athletics suspect that a large percentage of these kids are not having all that much fun. According to the article, this shouldn't be all that surprising. Practice schedules are often intense. Injuries are common and painful. Worst of all, there's the pressure.

Winning Isn't Everything

If you've ever seen a group of first graders on a soccer field, some will be kicking up dust, some may be pulling up clumps of grass, a couple may be watching the clouds. Most of them, when they're running around after the ball like a swarm of bees, are smiling and laughing. Winning or losing doesn't matter that much to them. One six-year-old boy named Mike, who had just finished playing a game in the rain and was clearly happy to be covered with mud, was asked, "Who won?"

He answered with a smile, "I don't know. Ask my mom or the coach."

To be sure, Mom and Dad know who won. The coaches know, too. Most of the kids just don't care. That's because at that young age, they still believe they are playing for fun. It's **unrealistic** to think that this totally relaxed level of play will continue. As kids become more **adept** at a sport and experience the **exhilaration** that comes with winning, it's natural that the desire to win becomes a **motivator**. With this new motivation comes a pressure to perform at a winning level. It's at this critical point that the tone of the game changes for many kids.

Completing a 5Ws web

Some of the 5Ws web for the first part of the magazine article has been filled in. Add more details. On a separate piece of paper, write a brief two-sentence or three-sentence summary for the first part of "Playing for the Fun of It."

Who? 30 million kids in elementary and high school sports

What? Competition pushes us to do better.

Topic/Main Idea
The increasing level of competitiveness in organized sports for children

Why? Intense practice schedules, injuries, and pressure

When?

Where?

Read the second part of the magazine article "Playing for the Fun of It."

Encouragement or Pressure

Encouragement is a good thing, especially when it is accompanied by love, understanding, and support. No one is suggesting that parents should not encourage their children to do their best at whatever sport they attempt. However, parents and coaches aren't always aware of the amount of pressure they are putting on their kids. For example, when parents decide to sell their home and move the whole family to a small apartment in another state so that they can afford figure skating lessons from a **renowned** instructor for their daughter, then it's not likely that the daughter is going to turn around and say, "You know, I don't think I like figure skating any more."

More and more children are enrolled in sports before they reach kindergarten age. Some kids begin playing a particular sport when they are three or four years old. By the time they're entering high school, if they're exceptionally good at the sport, parents and coaches begin talking about college scholarships. Kids start thinking, "Wow! I have to keep playing so that Mom and Dad don't have to worry about paying for my college."

Depending on the child's goals and the goals of parents and coaches, the pressure to win may begin to **outweigh** the pure fun of playing the game. Some kids decide they do not need that kind of pressure. In 2001, the National Alliance for Youth Sports reported that 70 percent of 13 years olds involved in organized sports in America had had enough. When asked why they quit, the kids responded, "It's just not fun anymore."

The Benefits of Sports Participation

Some kids actually thrive on competition and pressure. They are the kids who are constantly challenging themselves to do better. You may be one of these kids. For you and thousands of others who never get tired of playing the game, sports continues to offer physical and **psychological** benefits.

For one thing, any sport, whether it is an individual sport or a team sport, provides exercise. Exercise is a healthy **alternative** to sitting in front of the TV or a video game for hours. Exercise also releases endorphins. This chemical reaction in the brain creates a sense of overall well-being.

Sports also allow kids to **socialize** with other kids, not only from their own community but also from neighboring communities. When kids compete at higher levels, they may have the opportunity to travel around the country and, in some cases, around the world. When compared to sitting alone in front of the TV or a video game, participating in a sport would again seem to be the better choice.

Other important lessons that kids learn from sports can include the positive effects of teamwork and dedication to a goal, knowing when to lead as well as when to follow, and learning how to balance a busy schedule.

The founder of the Modern Day Olympics, Baron Pierre de Coubertin, said, "The important thing is not to win but to take part; the important thing in life is not the triumph but the struggle." If you enjoy the struggle and love participating in sports, then don't quit. Don't give up the benefits. However, if the pressure to win seems to be taking the fun out of the game, talk to your parents and tell them how you feel. Perhaps you can continue playing the sport at a less intense level, or maybe you'd like to try some other sport. Remember that parents want what is best for their children. And most children just want to have fun.

Using a 5Ws Web

Use facts and details from the second part of the magazine article to fill in the 5Ws web. If you want to create a web for each of the two headings, draw and complete a second 5Ws web on a separate piece of paper. Write your summary for the whole of part two on a separate piece of paper.

Who?

What?

Topic/Main Idea

Why?

When?

Where?

Check Your Understanding

Think about what you've read. Then answer these questions.

1. Which detail is not important enough to include in a summary of part one of "Playing for the Fun of It"?
   Ⓐ A 36-year-old football player is ready to retire.
   Ⓑ Approximately 30 million kids participate in organized sports programs.
   Ⓒ Athletic experts believe many kids are not having fun playing sports.
   Ⓓ Pressure changes the tone of the game for some kids.

2. According to the article, what do a ten-year-old baseball player and a 36-year-old professional football player have in common?
   Ⓐ They both wear cleats.
   Ⓑ They both play a rough sport.
   Ⓒ They both are too competitive.
   Ⓓ They both may be ready to retire.

3. Which of these is not a reason that experts give to explain why many kids aren't having fun playing sports?
   Ⓐ intense practice schedules
   Ⓑ frequent injuries
   Ⓒ TV and video games
   Ⓓ pressure

4. With a feeling of exhilaration, you would most likely
   Ⓐ jump with joy.
   Ⓑ want to go to sleep.
   Ⓒ express disappointment.
   Ⓓ quit what you're doing.

5. According to the author, at what critical point does the tone of playing a sport change for many kids?
   Ⓐ the first time someone asks, "Who won?"
   Ⓑ when they are repeatedly injured by their opponents
   Ⓒ the first time they lose a game
   Ⓓ when the desire to win begins to motivate their level of play

6. From the details in the article, you can conclude that the author believes that
   Ⓐ parents should not make sacrifices for their children to play sports.
   Ⓑ children should be able to decide at what level they want to play a sport.
   Ⓒ no child does well under pressure.
   Ⓓ competition has no place in youth sports.

7. If a player has no alternative, the player has no
   Ⓐ uniform.
   Ⓑ confidence.
   Ⓒ option.
   Ⓓ fun.

8. Which of these would provide the best opportunity for you to socialize?
   Ⓐ taking a test
   Ⓑ doing chores
   Ⓒ reading a book
   Ⓓ going to a party

9. What do you think will happen if the pressure to perform in youth sports gets more intense?
   Ⓐ A larger percentage of kids will quit playing sports.
   Ⓑ Parents will begin to complain about the pressure.
   Ⓒ More kids will receive college scholarships in athletics.
   Ⓓ Schools will eliminate all organized sports.

10. Which of these is the best summary of the section of the article titled "The Benefits of Sports Participation"?
    Ⓐ Some kids perform at a higher level as a result of pressure.
    Ⓑ Sports provides both physical and psychological benefits that kids won't get if they quit.
    Ⓒ Sports provides a wonderful opportunity for kids to meet other athletes.
    Ⓓ Parents want what is best for their children even if it doesn't always seem that way.

11. What is the article "Playing for the Fun of It" mostly about?

Ⓐ Children should not be encouraged to play sports at a competitive level.

Ⓑ Many kids thrive on competition and pressure.

Ⓒ The pressure to excel at a sport has taken the fun out of playing for many kids.

Ⓓ Only very young children enjoy playing sports because they don't care who wins or loses.

12. Why do you think the author wrote "Playing for the Fun of It"?

Ⓐ to entertain readers with a fun story about playing sports

Ⓑ to explain how to physically and psychologically get the most benefits out of playing a particular sport

Ⓒ to describe different sports

Ⓓ to remind readers that playing a sport should be fun and to persuade them not to quit without considering other options

Extend Your Learning

- *Write a Summary*

  Review the 5Ws web that you filled in as you read "Playing for the Fun of It," and look over the summary statements that you wrote for different parts of the article. You may also want to skim the article to refresh your memory and jot down additional facts and details in your 5Ws webs. Then put your ideas together to write a summary of the entire article. Compare your summary with those of your classmates.

- *Use a 5Ws Web to Read an Article*

  With a partner, find a newspaper or magazine article about a topic of interest to young people. For example, you might read an article about a new communications technology, a popular style of music, or any other topic of interest. Fill in a 5Ws web as you read the article. Then work together to create a summary using the facts and details in the web.

- *Engage in a Debate*

  With your classmates, prepare and perform a debate using this question as your topic: *Are organized sports for young people too competitive?* Divide into groups, so that each side of the argument is well represented. Use facts and details from the article "Playing for the Fun of It," and from other research to support your ideas.

Reading Selection One

Read the short story "Life in the City."

Life in the City

Elena Melissa Metropia Gonzales Smith stomped toward the park. The sun played with the tall buildings as she crossed the street. Once in the park, she moved past bright yellow daffodils and blue hyacinths, all neatly arranged in rows. Their scent was as sweet as honey. They looked as fragile as fine crystal. The flowers reminded her of the town where she used to live. Green was everywhere there.

She had had many friends at school, too. Not like here. She certainly wouldn't call the kids at school here friends. She hated going to the school because everyone made fun of her. The kids said her name was as distressingly long as she was tall, almost six feet in the sixth grade. It was awful being a new kid. And being so much taller than the other kids didn't help at all.

Her family had moved to the city a few months ago. As she walked through the park, the list of things she hated about her new life ran through her head over and over while her feet marched to the rhythm of the words, "I hate the buildings, I hate the streets, but most of all I hate the school."

As she slumped onto a park bench, she noticed a flock of pigeons milling around a lady who was throwing peanuts to them. The birds swarmed and clucked as they fought over the morsels. One pigeon with oddly colored spots that made it stand out from the others was constantly being pecked at and pushed away from the flock. Elena's attention was drawn to that bird and she thought, "That pigeon is like me. It doesn't look like the others." She smiled, then actually laughed aloud at the comparison. Then she noted the pigeon's behavior. This pigeon didn't shy away or leave the flock; it persistently tried to gain acceptance. Elena watched as it politely allowed other birds to pick up some of the peanuts that fell near it. No angry pushing or shoving for this bird, just quiet dignity as it mingled among the others. As Elena watched the patient pigeon, she made a new plan for her own behavior. Maybe she could make things different at school. And with friends, maybe life in the city wouldn't be so bad after all.

Check Your Understanding

Think about what you've read. Then answer these questions.

1. Why does Elena dislike going to her new school?
   A There are no flowers at the school.
   B She has no friends at the new school.
   C Her classmates are too short.
   D She only likes the company of pigeons.

2. Which sentence from the story does not include a figure of speech?
   A The sun played with the tall buildings as she crossed the street.
   B Their scent was as sweet as honey.
   C They looked as fragile as fine crystal.
   D Once in the park, she moved past bright yellow daffodils and blue hyacinths, all neatly arranged in rows.

3. What do you predict might happen if the story continued?
   A Elena will try again to make friends at school.
   B Elena will visit the town she used to live in.
   C Elena will run away from home.
   D Elena will live in the park with the pigeons.

4. Why does Elena think that she is like the spotted pigeon?
   A Elena and the spotted pigeon both have freckles.
   B Elena and the spotted pigeon both stand out as different.
   C Elena and the spotted pigeon both behave the same way.
   D Elena and the spotted pigeon both like the park.

5. The main purpose of this story is to
   A entertain the reader and suggest a lesson.
   B persuade the reader to go for a walk in the park.
   C describe a beautiful flower garden.
   D explain how to make friends.

6. How was Elena's school in town different from the one in the city?
   A The school in town had green grass around it, but the city school does not.
   B In the town school, the students were the same height as Elena, but in the city school, they are shorter.
   C Elena liked school in the town because she had friends, but in the city she has been unable to make friends.
   D The sun shines on the city school while the school in the town was in shade.

7. The sentences below list events from the story.
   1 Elena walks to the park.
   2 Elena sees a spotted pigeon.
   3 Elena complains about her new life.
   4 Elena sits down on a park bench.
   Which of these is the right order?
   A 4, 2, 1, 3
   B 3, 1, 2, 4
   C 1, 3, 4, 2
   D 1, 4, 3, 2

8. The main idea, or theme, of the story is
   A animals have more feelings than people.
   B kind people feed the pigeons.
   C sometimes you have to make a special effort to gain friends.
   D people should never move.

9. In the end, why does Elena decide to behave differently at school?
   A She watches a patient pigeon that doesn't give up trying to be accepted.
   B She sees flowers that make her feel better.
   C The woman feeding the pigeons is kind.
   D She changes her mind about life in the city.

10. What does Elena dislike most about her new life?
    A the streets   C the pigeons
    B the school   D the tall buildings

Read the how-to article "Let the Play Begin!"

Let the Play Begin!

Suppose you and a friend want to direct a play. You will need to consider all aspects of drama to present a real play. Yet, if you follow through with the time and effort, you will have fun, get to know more people, learn a lot, and maybe make some money for your school, club, or classroom.

First, find a play you want to direct. You can find some plays for performing in collections at the library. You can write your own play or adapt a story (such as a fable or novel) into play form. If you use someone else's play or adapt an author's story, get permission if you plan to charge money for your play.

Once you've decided on your play, begin casting. Put up posters announcing auditions and/or talk to students in your school. You will find many eager thespians! Plan auditions so that each hopeful will have about five minutes to read a part. Thank everyone for coming. As directors, you and your friend decide who will play which part. Consider how well the person read the lines and how well he or she fits the part. You wouldn't want a boisterous person to play a gentle butterfly, or a small, quiet person to play a noisy giant.

Give a script to each selected player. Distribute a rehearsal schedule. First, have a read through where the players sit and read their lines. Everyone discusses the play and how they think the characters could be best shown. At the following rehearsals, get the players up on stage, moving according to the stage directions in the script—and having fun! Make sure players face the audience and speak loudly. Since not all stage directions are written in the script, you will have to do more blocking. For blocking, you sketch out what each player will do on the stage. You decide where the player will stand or sit, enter or exit. You establish exactly how the player will move. Assign a date when everyone must have their lines memorized. Then practice, practice, practice!
Once rehearsals are running well, begin detailing. Work with each scene to get every detail of expression and movement into place. Then practice, practice, practice!

At the same time, you need lots of people who don't want to act but do want to help. Select a technical crew to run the lights, open and close the curtains, play music, and/or create sound effects. Gather a team to help design and make the sets, or scenery for the stage. Keep the plans simple and creative. Look for ways to make scenery out of paper, cardboard boxes, lightweight wood, and cloth. Make accurate and specific drawings before you paint sets. For the performances, select dependable stage hands to move the background sets and furniture on and off the stage between scenes. They will have to know exactly where everything goes—and when!

Another team can plan and create costumes, including makeup. You don't need to have elaborate costumes to create interesting effects. White sweat pants, a shirt, painted paper ears, and a rope tail could make a cute mouse. An oversized men's suit coat might suggest an adult businessman.

Set up a small team for props. A prop, or property, is anything used by a player on stage: a comb, newspaper, water glass, basket, broom, and so on. The prop team makes or gathers the needed props. For the performance, the team places props on a prop table in the wings. The team has covered the table with paper and outlined each prop. When an actress needs a prop, she picks it up from the table. When she is done, she puts it back inside its outline.

The stage manager and assistants are important backstage workers. Set up a prompt copy for the stage manager. This copy has a page of script on the right and directions for actors, lighting, and sound on the left. The prompt copy is valuable. It is useful to keep rehearsals running smoothly and to prompt players and crew, if they need it, during the performance.

Have the crew come to several rehearsals to practice. In a "tech" rehearsal, the technical crew supported by the stage managers run through their tasks. In a dress rehearsal, everyone experiences the play, in costume, just as if it were the real thing.

If you are putting the play on for the community, don't forget to let people know. Put up posters and/or contact the local newspaper. Remember to make a program, or playbill, for the performance and get a front-of-house team to sell tickets and pass out playbills.

Check Your Understanding

Think about what you've read. Then answer these questions.

11. Which sentence is not a detail the author mentions about the benefits of putting on a play?
    Ⓐ You could learn a lot.
    Ⓑ You could make some money.
    Ⓒ You could become famous.
    Ⓓ You could have fun.

12. Select the correct sequence of the following activities as outlined in the article.
    A=read through, B=blocking, C=casting, D=detailing
    Ⓐ A, B, C, D
    Ⓑ D, C, A, B
    Ⓒ C, A, B, D
    Ⓓ C, A, D, B

13. During performances, what is the purpose of the outlines on the prop table?
    Ⓐ to make sure no props are too large for the stage
    Ⓑ to show players what the props should look like
    Ⓒ to make the table more attractive
    Ⓓ to make it easy to see if any props are missing

14. What is the meaning of the word *thespians* in the third paragraph on page 126?
    Ⓐ actors
    Ⓑ teachers
    Ⓒ people who read posters
    Ⓓ people who want to attend the play

15. How does detailing compare to blocking?
    Ⓐ Detailing is for the crew, but blocking is for the players.
    Ⓑ Detailing is for rehearsals while blocking is for performances.
    Ⓒ Detailing is more specific and fine-tuned than blocking.
    Ⓓ Detailing is written into the play but blocking isn't.

16. Which of these is the best summary for this article?
    Ⓐ A play requires actors. If they are good at memorizing, they will not have to work so hard to do a good job.
    Ⓑ Directing a play begins with choosing the play and ends with the performance. Participants work hard in between.
    Ⓒ Putting on a play is one way to learn about theater. It can prepare you to study more about stage and screen when you're older.
    Ⓓ To present a play, you need to have fancy scenery and costumes. That way, you can charge money for your play.

17. The main purpose of this article is to
    Ⓐ entertain you with an interesting story about a play.
    Ⓑ persuade you to become a play director.
    Ⓒ describe the sets and costumes for a play.
    Ⓓ explain the steps needed to put on a play.

18. Which of these statements is a fact?
    Ⓐ The prop team makes or gathers the needed props.
    Ⓑ The prompt copy is valuable.
    Ⓒ You don't need to have elaborate costumes to create interesting effects.
    Ⓓ The stage manager and assistants are important backstage workers.

19. Which of these could be another title for this article?
    Ⓐ "How to Put On a Play"
    Ⓑ "Casting for a Play"
    Ⓒ "Tips for Great Play Writing"
    Ⓓ "A Perfect Schoolwide Project"

20. What do you think the author would discuss if the article continued?
    Ⓐ how to memorize lines for a play
    Ⓑ where to buy materials for sets
    Ⓒ how to manage the performance
    Ⓓ when to announce the play to the community